WHAT XAVIERA HAS TO SAY ABOUT THE BEST PART OF A MAN WILL MAKE EVERY MAN STAND UP—AND PAY ATTENTION!

Now the Happy Hooker lays it all on the line to share the joy of sex with you, re-creating the lessons she's taught as well as the equally fascinating lessons she's learned in her intimate dealings with—

The Best Part of a Man

SIGNET Books You'll Enjoy Reading

☐ **THE MAKING OF THE HAPPY HOOKER by Robin Moore.** Now it can be told—the inside story of how Xaviera Hollander switched from "hook" to "book" to become a literary sensation. And what an inside story it is, complete with the most kinky, inhibited goings on and loads of titillating sensual adventures. (#W5662—$1.50)

☐ **SEX PARLOR by Larry Kleinman.** Sex Parlor leaves nothing out in the most unblushing, straight-talking expose ever printed of how far professional sex has come today in a phenomenon that is now spreading from city to suburb, over the entire country! Included are eight pages of explicit photographs. (#W5685—$1.50)

☐ **THE SEX INDUSTRY by George Csicsery.** A sex-pose of happy hookers, massage parlors, skin flicks—every kick money can buy! (#Y5641—$1.25)

☐ **TRICKS OF THE TRADE: A Hooker's Handbook of Sexual Technique by John Warren Wells.** Nine call girls candidly reveal what it is like to be a prostitute, how they came into the business and why they stay. (#Q5350—95¢)

☐ **GENTLEMAN OF LEISURE: A Year in the Life of a Pimp,** text by Susan Hall; photographed by Bob Adelman. The pimp who makes more money than the President of the United States tells the shocking, intimate story of his profession—with explicit photographs of his world—and his women. (#J5524—$1.95)

THE NEW AMERICAN LIBRARY, INC.,
P.O. Box 999, Bergenfield, New Jersey 07621

Please send me the SIGNET BOOKS I have checked above. I am enclosing $_____(check or money order—no currency or C.O.D.'s). Please include the list price plus 25¢ a copy to cover handling and mailing costs. (Prices and numbers are subject to change without notice.)

Name_____

Address_____

City_____State_____Zip Code_____
Allow at least 3 weeks for delivery

XAVIERA ON THE BEST PART OF A MAN

by
Xaviera Hollander

A BERNARD GEIS ASSOCIATES BOOK

A SIGNET BOOK
NEW AMERICAN LIBRARY
TIMES MIRROR

Copyright © 1975 by Artistae Stiftung

Cover photographs by Michael Brennan

*All rights reserved. For information address
Bernard Geis Associates, Inc., 128 East 56th Street,
New York, New York 10022.*

Published by arrangement with Bernard Geis Associates, Inc.

SIGNET TRADEMARK REG. U.S. PAT. OFF. AND FOREIGN COUNTRIES
REGISTERED TRADEMARK—MARCA REGISTRADA
HECHO EN CHICAGO, U.S.A.

SIGNET, SIGNET CLASSICS, MENTOR, PLUME AND MERIDIAN BOOKS
are published by The New American Library, Inc.,
1301 Avenue of the Americas, New York, New York 10019

FIRST PRINTING, JULY, 1975

3 4 5 6 7 8 9

PRINTED IN THE UNITED STATES OF AMERICA

Contents

1. The Penis: The Long and the Short of It — 1
2. Playing the Pink Piccolo, or, The Glory of "O" — 9
3. Masturbation: I. A Handbook — 29
4. Masturbation: II. *Mit Fantasies* — 44
5. The Erector Set, or, The Adolescent Penis — 51
6. Top Banana at the Orgy — 68
7. The Sign of the Cock: Your Sexual Horoscope — 83
8. Circumcision: The Kindest Cut of All — 103
9. Ten Ways to Pleasure the Penis, or, Ladies, the Ball's in Your Court — 113
10. A Pleasure Chest of Sex Toys, or, Try These for Openers — 138
11. A Treasury of Orgasms, or, How to Come in Nine Languages — 155
12. Getting Your Money's Worth in a Brothel, or, Joint Negotiations — 168
13. Exotic Penises I Have Known, or, Oddballs, Perky Pricks, and Other Strange Bedfellows — 181

14. Keep It Clean as a Whistle or
    It Won't Get Blown   203
15. My Life and Soft Times, or,
    The Reluctant Penis   211
16. Sex Appeal Seventies Style, or,
    My Most Penetrating Performers   227

CHAPTER ONE

The Penis: The Long and the Short of It

As a woman who has enjoyed love with both sexes, I find that there is nothing in the world that comes up to the penis. I have had a lot of loving homosexual relationships and still do. But what they lack is a good healthy penis, which I still prefer to anything else—above any girl, animal, or device, even above myself. A woman can have sex by masturbating with a vibrator or dildo or any other innovation. But nothing can substitute for the penis of warm and living flesh.

To me, the penis seems like an independent organ of the male body—attached to the man, but belonging to both him and to me. It is shared, like a mutual friend between lovers, to be enjoyed by them both during lovemaking. It has a mind of its own: *he* can be asleep and *it* can decide to have an erection. It has a memory that can be trained and conditioned in such techniques as delaying or hastening ejaculation. It is highly teachable.

The first erect penis I ever saw was my father's as he gave my mother a loving hug in our bathroom. I became immediately fascinated by the male organ and wished I had one like it. This does not mean that I feel incomplete as a woman. At least, not any longer.

The day I acquired my first male lover, who shared his penis with me—and very gladly—I got my childhood wish. And I've been getting it ever since.

Mutual ownership of a penis, however, is only the first step. Both partners must learn what to do with it. And here, I must say, the man is more likely to be at fault than the woman. Too many men think that if they have a big cock they are automatically the world's best lover, which is not the case, because the man may be selfish or unskilled and not please the woman at all. He's like the beautiful men or women who have never seen the need to develop any faculties beyond their physical endowments and who are consequently dull and boring. We all know what happened to Narcissus—he ended up being his only best friend.

Since my first book, *The Happy Hooker*, was published, I have received thousands and thousands of letters. Far too many of them come from women complaining that their men don't know how to please them—that the women are horny and excited but finally have to resort to masturbation because the man is too self-centered. He thinks his lovemaking responsibility is fulfilled by letting her shake hands with the devil from time to time, especially if he happens to have a big dick.

Male preoccupation with the size of the penis is obsessive and often irrational. Obviously, if he is a "pencil case" he will have to shape up and compensate, or maybe get his name in the *Guinness Book of World Records* as the world's best "cunnilinguist" or "handyman." But it is a myth—and one of the many that will be laid to rest in this book—that size, in sex, is everything.

Preoccupation with size, however, is hardly limited to the male of the species. For example, a psychiatrist told me a story of a woman who rejected her husband's lovemaking because she believed that when it came to the penis, he just did not measure up. As a result, their marriage was falling apart.

She had an inflated idea of adequate endowment from a glimpse she had caught of her father's erect penis when she was a little girl and he had accidentally allowed his robe to fall open. "How big was your father's penis?" the psychiatrist asked her. "This big," she said, demonstrating with her hands held apart. He took out a yardstick and measured the distance. It was twenty inches. "Are you absolutely sure it was this big?" he asked.

"Well, *this* big," she said, reducing the space to fourteen inches.

"No such size," the psychiatrist said, "unless it's on a horse."

After more deliberation, she became realistic and held her hands six inches apart. "Actually, I guess it was really this size," she said, de-spooking the fallacy and giving her literally "penalized" husband a break at last.

Generally speaking, bigger is not better, just different. During my life as a professional and as a lover I have seen so many penises that I have lost count. I've discovered that every man, just as he has a distinctive face, has also a different penis, and every one of them is fascinating and exciting in its own way. One has a cute one, another has a tremendously long one, someone else has a stubby one, another has a slightly bent one, one has a strong one that holds out for hours, just like a fucking machine, and yet another has an impatient little bugger that has a rhythm all its own with a dynamite charge at the climax.

Of course, size is especially irrelevant if the penis is reluctant to stand up and be counted. Impotence, or the inability to "get it up," is so widespread in America today that in the last four years alone five thousand sex clinics have sprung up to deal with that which refuses to do likewise. Impotence is an invisible epidemic against which you can't be immunized, though at least it's not contagious.

At fashionable Manhattan parties these days it is considered provocative to tell a pretty girl, "I can't get it up anymore." She is supposed to take this as a challenge to try to persuade his reluctant organ to stand up and take notice of her femininity. But all too often it has become a self-fulfilling prophecy.

The penis is a temperamental instrument, and it is connected to an even more temperamental part of the anatomy—the brain. Impotence, real or imaginary, is one of the main problems I've learned to cope with. During my years as a professional I've seen thousands of men go through my house and into my body. I've heard their problems and tried to help them. Somehow I have always felt attracted to people with problems—not necessarily losers in life, but vulnerable people. I like to make them feel at ease and satisfy their sexual needs.

While I was a madam I worked with several psychiatrists on a regular basis in New York. They sometimes referred their sexual problem cases to me. The doctors believed that, while they had studied and learned all the theories about masochism, sadism, fetishism, child molesting, and homosexuality, they were still lacking in practical application. And it is true that behind all the technical names and learned mumbo-jumbo, only a girl like me with lots of front-line experience can spot the real troublemaker in a sex problem. It is usually a penis that won't. My job has been to retrain a reluctant organ into giving the heads-up performance of which it is capable—unless, of course, there's a real physical disability, which is rarely the case.

I remember a young homosexual Catholic boy who was referred to me. His entire upbringing was directed toward his marrying and having children. He desperately wanted to fulfill his parents' wishes, but he could not. He was perfectly well equipped, but though I tried every titillating trick in the book it was like flogging a dead horse. There was no flicker of response. Then I realized that first I had to make this young man appreciate a woman's body, which I did by simply lying beside him nude in order to teach him to relax and get acquainted with the other sex. I suspected he was not going to get a hard-on the first day, and I was right. It took three sessions, but eventually he was no longer scared and started to take the initiative and make advances to me. When that little soldier finally stood up and saluted, I knew the battle was won.

I have helped, through person-to-person contact, through letters or at lectures, many thousands of people with sexual problems. I have also served as a consultant on the staff of Clark Institute of Psychiatry in Toronto. My work as a consultant, lecturer, and teacher in the field of sex instruction has been as educational to me, in a way, as it has been to those I taught. It has exposed to me, far more than my experiences in the bedroom (because it's the men who are far too shy to enter my "house" who need the most help; and women seldom enter it except professionally, and Lord knows some of them know more about the birds and bees than I do), the vast and harmful ignorance that still prevails on the subject of good, healthy sex. That is the main reason, in fact, that I've written this book.

I was amazed at the number and types of questions people asked, for example, on over a hundred radio hotline shows I conducted. It seems the anonymity of the radio made them open up and reveal what was on their minds, in their hearts, and in their beds. I have lectured to college audiences of one and two thousand students between the ages of eighteen and twenty-five, and have been surprised and delighted at their straightforwardness and eagerness to learn.

In more intimate groups there have been housewives, young couples who knew only too well they were sexually illiterate, and larger professional groups, including lawyers, social workers, psychologists, business executives, and convention delegates.

Because my special insight was acquired through experience, doctors have invited me to hold discussions on all kinds of subjects they felt would supplement their theoretical knowledge. There have been many psychotherapy groups, in which the psychiatrist presented the case history of the person with the sexual problem and we would all talk together very openly and helpfully.

Strictly and literally speaking, I could be classified as a lay analyst, because when it comes to sex therapy, I have no formal degree. However, what counts, I believe, is what works. Sex therapy, although very important now, is still in its infancy, and nobody is too organized about it yet. "Sex therapy is where medicine was around the turn of the century," says Dr. William Masters. Because of this and the fact that sex has become a "hot consumer item," the profession has its share of Dr. Snake Oils hanging around.

According to Dr. Masters, of the five thousand sex clinics operating today, only about fifty do any good. "The public is being incredibly bilked," he says. But at least people are finally buying the idea that sex is a natural function and that problems should not be swept under the mattress.

This all leads up to the subject of this book—the emancipation of the penis through the emancipation of the mind. If the brain doesn't send a message to the penis, the penis won't perform. And if the penis doesn't perform, our sex lives could all be one big zero. Therefore, this book is about the penis and all that is connected with it, for both men and women, and from both points of view. I hope it gives everyone a bigger and better lift. That's the whole point of the book—and the penis.

It seems strange that although there are medical texts on the subject, nobody has yet done a popular but serious work on the male sex organ. After all, its a rather important part of the human anatomy. As my friend Warren Brock has pointed out:

> We wouldn't have Alice
> Without someone's phallus.

And yet there seems to be a conspiracy of silence on the subject. Think of how many books there are on the heart! But not a single one on an organ that is not only far more fascinating but just as important, since without it there wouldn't be a human race. Well, here's that book. And if I do say so myself, it couldn't have been written by a better-qualified person.

Just one word of warning: fasten your seat belt tightly. Xaviera doesn't beat around the bush!

CHAPTER TWO

Playing the Pink Piccolo, OR, The Glory of "O"

Cleopatra conquered emperors with it, Linda Lovelace captured audiences with it, the seductive women of Bologna made an industry of it, and in my New York establishment, I made a big business out of it.

It's called fellatio, going down, giving head, playing the pink piccolo, plating, sucking, *soixante-neuf*, or, in its most endearing form, a blowjob. And men love it so much that when I ran New York's most successful brothel at least eighty percent of my customers requested oral sex, mostly because their wives wouldn't or couldn't do it.

Although oral sex is such a normal activity to the younger generation that many of them become expert at it even before they have actually engaged in heterosexual intercourse, there's still a whole society of sexually active couples in their mid-thirties and over who don't know what it is all about, or are too timid to find out. When I was in England once I met a nice-looking father of five who was sophisticated, charming, and a widely traveled foreign correspondent on a Fleet Street newspaper. At the age of forty-two he had never experienced having his cock sucked by his wife or anyone else.

Then one time his newspaper sent him on assignment to India with some of his colleagues, and they all decided to treat him to a no-strings-attached blowjob in a local brothel. As they stood in line being sucked, one by one, by the dusky young prostitutes, his religious principles and hang-ups started to nag him, and he became nervous and restless. By the time his turn came around, he was so confused and embarrassed that he started insulting the astonished girl and stormed angrily out of the place. To this day, as far as I know, he has never experienced the glory of "O."

It is testimony to the unnecessary sexual chaos in people's lives that every week, among the hundreds of letters I receive, six out of ten are about oral-sex problems. This might seem surprising to those of us who accept fellatio as being as much a part of our love lives as conversation. One woman wrote:

Dear Xaviera:
After twenty-two years of reasonably happy marriage, I have reached the painful conclusion that I have to learn to perform oral sex with my husband or stand helplessly by and see him stray with a more liberal woman. I tried it once, but my deep-seated fears and inhibitions got in the way and I was so clumsy I bit his penis. He has hinted now he is justified in seeking oral pleasure elsewhere and insists it will not harm our marriage. Should I believe him? What should I do?

Tongue-Tied
St. Louis, Mo.

My answer:

In his opinion, he has a perfect right to seek elsewhere the lip service he isn't paid at home. But if you swallow that, you'll swallow anything. You'd better learn—and learn fast. Never underestimate the value of a competent blowjob.

If a woman is incapable of the act of fellatio, believe me, the problem is in her mind, not in her esophagus or any other part of her anatomy. Who can ever forget the WASP socialite in Philip Roth's *Portnoy's Complaint*? True, she finally managed to hold Portnoy's cock in her mouth for sixty seconds, "like a thermometer." But that was as far as she could bring herself to go. She was sure she would suffocate if she continued, and it was useless to attempt to explain that it's possible to breathe through one's nose even with that big obstruction in one's mouth. Finally, Portnoy gave up because he suddenly visualized the lurid headline: "JEW SMOTHERS DEB WITH COCK; VASSAR GRAD GEORGETOWN STRANGULATION VICTIM; MOCKY LAWYER HELD."

The dazzling and passionate Cleopatra was aware of the value of mouth power, and it is erotic history that the tempestuous queen of the Nile was one of the world's all-time great fellatrixes. She obviously caught on quickly that you don't make loving slaves out of powerful emperors by being prim in bed. And there is a city in northern Italy so famous for the cock-sucking skills of its voluptuous women that, even to this day, you can still pick up a copy of Rome's most respected mass-circulation dailies and find thinly disguised advertisements in the classified section reading: "Massage given, Bolognese style." It is perhaps more than a coincidence that bologna, the sausage that's so good to eat, derives its name from that selfsame city.

Possibly the most celebrated practitioner of the blowjob of all is the mandibular Linda Lovelace, who is to fellatio what Olga Korbut is to the parallel bars—minus the Olympic recognition. In her controversial movie, *Deep Throat,* which perhaps should have been named *Sore Throat,* she broke box-office records and even triggered a move to restructure an entire obscenity code when she performed her spectacular sword-swallowing act.

I'm certainly not a prude, as everyone knows, but I was really turned off by her act, which I thought was just too much and too gross, especially with all the saliva coming out of her mouth, the snot out of her nose, and the sperm all over her cheeks as she was impaled on the penis like a man-eating shish-kebab. I always considered sperm healthy and full of protein once swallowed, although I don't happen to like the taste. But as a facial cream it's not in the same class as Elizabeth Arden. Not only that, watching ninety minutes of a girl going through the same monotonous activity was boring and just not a turn-on. Her throat-fucking act may be her gig, but it is more of a gimmick than a satisfying or artistic blowjob.

The trouble with the Linda Lovelace publicity was that men all over the country started demanding that their girlfriends and wives learn how to do a blowjob, which is not too difficult but can be dangerous. Many people each year actually choke to death at meals when objects that are considerably smaller than an excited penis get stalled in their throats. Maybe I'm an alarmist, however; after all, the penis *does* have a rather large handle attached to it, in the shape of a man, with which it can be withdrawn at the first sign of trouble.

I learned the deep-throat technique to please my lover, but it took me weeks to perfect it without gagging. To prepare to take a penis deep in her throat, a woman first has to teach herself to overcome the involuntary sensation of wanting to gag when a foreign object is introduced. You have to practice finger-stroking behind the tongue until you succeed, which is like a yoga exercise, in a way. Next, many people get dizzy hanging their heads lower than their bodies, so this has to be overcome too, since the mouth and throat have to be in a straight line so that the penis can go down.

When the woman thinks she can take it, she lies face-up on the bed, head hanging over the edge, with the man kneeling in front of her face. In the same way he penetrates her for anal intercourse, slowly and gently and little by little, he starts inserting his penis. To make matters more complicated, the woman can breathe only on each withdrawal stroke.

All in all, as you can see, it requires quite a technique. It's up to you to decide whether it's worth it. I asked my lover whether he really liked it, and he said seeing me swallow his entire penis in the ceiling mirror was more exciting than feeling it. So it was more of a psychological trip than a physical one, not that I'm knocking psychology, especially when all else fails.

Actually, like most men, my lover preferred me to have a firm grip with my mouth around the upper part of his penis, because when I put my mouth all the way down to the base, there was none of the stimulating feeling of suction at the tip, where nearly all men have their greatest sensitivity. In the penis, the most sensitive parts are the cap, the corona—or rim—and the top of the shaft just under the rim, where eighty percent of the nerve endings are concentrated. The really excitable part is the frenulum, the little knot in the circumcised penis or the join between shaft and cap in the uncircumcised penis, which can be located by gently pulling back the foreskin.

Men, and especially their penises (I still think of the penis as a separate "person"), like fellatio so much that I really believe many, if not most, have at least one time in their lives attempted a blowjob on themselves. Many animals, such as chimpanzees, rhesus monkeys, and other mammals, actually suck their own cocks. But for all except very supple and dedicated human vertebrates, this is an anatomical impossibility. There were three men in the Kinsey report who admitted they made a lifelong pastime of self-fellatio, but I believe that men who desire to suck their own cocks are likely to become homosexuals, or at least have strong homosexual inclinations. It seems logical that if they enjoy the idea of sucking their own penis, they would enjoy sucking someone else's.

According to Freud, the first organ to make its appearance as an "erotogenic zone" and to make libidinal demands upon the mind is, from the time of birth onward, the mouth. In time, and given the appropriate neurotic environment, some men become so oral-genital-fixated about themselves that they turn into hopeless freaks. I had a regular customer in New York, a very square Jewish businessman, who, under the effects of amyl nitrate, had a compulsion to suck himself off. To do this he had to lie on his back with his legs swung up over his head, resting on the wall behind him. But as hard as he tried to insert his penis into his mouth, there was still a stubborn five inches between the organ and his eager orifice. So he would ejaculate by jacking himself off, and for him the great turn-on was seeing himself come in his mouth. But the moment he did, he would snap out of it and start spitting out his sperm and become very disgusted. Needless to say, the next time he came back, he would do the whole thing over again.

A generation ago, as far as the general population was aware, fellatio was an Italian baritone. If you told someone it was the opposite of cunnilingus, you would only be piling confusion on bewilderment. Kinsey did a survey years ago that showed that the upper classes indulged in cocksucking much more than their less privileged—educationally and financially—brothers and sisters. In the latest sex surveys, although more lovers are enjoying it, this class and education difference still persists, possibly because of deep-seated superstitions and taboos.

I say: Down with class discrimination and down with sex taboos. I feel it is my duty to point out that there is no mystery to a good blowjob. Fellatio knows no class barrier, and you do not need a college degree to suck a cock. (Just take a lesson from Hollander's College of Carnal Knowledge.) Not only that, you're never too old to learn. Neither do you need to be an acrobat of the esophagus like Linda Lovelace.

For the purpose of this lesson, let's assume there is one basic blowjob from which arise (if you'll pardon the expression) all the erotic variations. These depend on position, pressure, speed, wetness, and the like. For example, one penis may not tolerate a firm grip, while another might lose its head over it. Another penis likes it barely moist, while still another likes you slobbering all over the place so that it swims in saliva.

The perfect blowjob should first of all be a combination of a really fast tongue, together with a succulent mouth that has a sense of imagination. Two movements, either independently, or together if you're really adept, are basic. They are the up-and-down with lips *tightened* to resemble the entrance of a snug vagina; and the other is the flicking of the tongue, left to right, especially around the rim. I have trained my tongue to vibrate so fast that men tell me it is literally the fastest tongue in the East. However, despite what you may have read in this or that sex book, there is no such thing as an exercise to train the tongue. It's a case of learning by doing. You can, however, also experiment on your lover's tongue during mouth-kissing.

Certainly the speed of the tongue depends on the desires of the man, just as it does with a woman. When I am eating pussy, I have discovered that there are girls who like the languid, gentle tongue on or around their clitoris; others prefer it fast; and the same applies to a man. You can adjust your tongue and mouth movements by gathering from his responses what turns him on.

If you are both in a frisky, playful mood, there is a

game that is a perfect indicator of what excites the penis most. It is like painting by numbers, except I guess you'd call it sucking by numbers. On a scale of ten, as you suck, lick, and flick, the man has to tell you the stimulation quotient. The greater the sensation, the higher the number. That way, you not only get feedback, as it were, on how it feels, but you also vary your lovemaking technique. In terms of how it feels to the penis, the woman can compare the sensation of the head to the sensation she's familiar with on her clitoris, and can identify the sensation of her manipulating his scrotum to that of his doing likewise to her vulva or labia. It's not as complicated as it sounds, once you're on the actual playing field.

A very erotic area for the man during oral sex is obviously the scrotum, particularly if the balls are gently licked, and especially when taken, one at a time, into the mouth. The bridge between the scrotum and anus—the perineum—is a high-count erogenous zone, and if touched properly, which can be done with more pressure than on the balls, it is a tremendous turn-on for the man.

At all times while sucking your lover's penis, make sure you do not use your teeth too vigorously, or you might accidentally bite his cock when he thrusts it deep into your throat. I did this quite hard once when I was very young and inexperienced, and I would not be surprised if the man involved has never had the courage to put his penis in another mouth since. It's a rare organ that does not have a deep and abiding fear of castration. A lot of my letters are from men complaining that their wives bite them. On the other hand, there are some penises that respond ecstatically to occasional gentle nips.

Going beyond this, if the man is in a slightly masochistic mood, as most of us occasionally are, you can use your teeth in a certain way that can be very exciting. You hold the penis sideways in your mouth, like a harmonica—or should I say mouth organ?—and, together with the tongue and the teeth, you sort of stimulate the whole shaft up to the head, back and forth, like eating corn on the cob, giving it light, harmless nibbles; it should be more like, say, a scratching of the fingernails lightly on the surface of his back, rather than a digging in of your claws.

Giving a fully enjoyable blowjob without using your hands would be like dancing without a partner. It can be done, but it's not very enjoyable. It's literally giving lip service instead of the genuine article. You can do a lot to increase the intensity of his pleasure manually, gently massaging the shaft as though masturbating it, as well as touching up the scrotum and the anus. I usually make sure I have one short fingernail so I can wet it with my saliva or a lubricant and insert it in his anus while giving him a blowjob. This is also a secret a lot of hookers use to make the customer come quicker if he is a slow ejaculator, which happens often if he is tired or has been drinking excessively and cannot concentrate on reaching an orgasm. Professionals overcome this by putting one finger all the way into the anus, probing around to locate the prostate gland, then massaging this back and forth, which seems to be the trigger-puller for quick ejaculation.

There is also the reverse situation, which is when you want to delay the ejaculation because you don't want the penis to discharge in your mouth. Unless I really care for a man, or unless we have a mutual orgasm during sixty-nine and I am excited to distraction, I don't generally want to swallow his come. I have seldom tasted sperm that was not bitter, though I realize many women feel quite differently. Whatever you do, if by accident or design he comes in your mouth, *never* react with obvious distaste. If you can manage it gracefully, go into the bathroom and spit the sperm out; if not, turn on your side in bed and let it leak from the side of your mouth, preferably into a tissue or washcloth if you have one handy. If your man really wants you to swallow his come, make sure you do so in one big gulp. This reduces the taste, because it bypasses the taste buds located in the front of the tongue.

Let's say, however, you don't mind swallowing semen, and, in fact, even like it. There still may be two other reasons for wanting to delay orgasm during fellatio. One might be for the purpose of tantalizing the penis as an erotic exercise, and the other because the eager organ suffers from bouts of hair-trigger trouble.

The first, and possibly the easiest, stop-the-pop method for most lovers to try, especially if they are learners, is the so-called "squeeze technique." It is applied by the woman, who squeezes the top of the shaft really tight between her thumb and forefinger. She does it when he is just about at the paradise stroke, and it is such a torture for the man that the penis will usually continue to go up and down if it is still in her mouth.

How do you know if he is almost at the point of no return? If a woman is a sensitive lover, she can feel the penis growing thicker and really rigid like steel and the veins getting more pronounced. She has the added advantage of more sensitivity in her tongue than in her vagina; also, the balls will get tight and go inside the body, and the man will usually start moaning and groaning.

There is a modification of the squeeze technique that would probably be called *lingus interruptus,* if it had a name, which is what I did to my lover recently and cost myself a good screw because of it. Before making love, he told me, "I want to come inside your body and not in your mouth." So each time I brought him almost to the brink of orgasm, I pulled away and left him cliff-hanging. After doing this three times, which is a sort of agony-ecstasy for the man, you condition the penis and program the ejaculation mechanism to be "inoperative," as they say in the White House. He won't really get soft, but he will have a difficult time making love to conclusion.

Another, more elaborate method of slowing penis ejaculation during oral sex is to put the organ into restrictive bondage. You take some surgical cord, which is actually elastic but not the thin rubber band that would cut into the flesh, and tie it around the head of the penis *after* it is erect. When the penis is beautifully trussed, it gets as hard as a rock and it cannot go down, and you can suck it until the penis goes out of its head, because it is almost impossible for it to ejaculate until released.

There are gadgets on the market that look like rubber rings and are used around the base of the penis, as well as the balls, for the same orgasm-inhibiting effect; but the surgical cord is easier to find, and better for those who prefer things less contrived. When you tie it, make sure the cord is firm so that the penis gets a numbing feeling, but not so tight that it's painful or dangerous. In any kind of bondage scene, whether it's wrists and/or ankles, never leave your lover tied up for more than half an hour. In the case of the penis, it will change color from pinkish to almost purplish if it's too tight, and if it gets dark, you know it's time to unleash your man.

While a woman is performing a blowjob on her man, there are lots of added gourmet delicacies she can apply if she is imaginative and resourceful—things she can put in her mouth to make the sexual texture different and more exciting. Ice has incredible shock value on a penis, or if this is too frosty, chilled air blowing onto it from a mouth full of ice. My suggestion for a natural way of doing it is when you're relaxing with a drink and the ice is right there in the glasses. Many men and women are uncomfortable about variations and experiments in sex that are not spontaneous, and they tend to feel silly contriving them. But while the mood is relaxed and sensual and the ice is at hand, she can either roll it around in her mouth just long enough to make her tongue chilled or keep crushed ice or an ice cube in her mouth while blowing him. She can stimulate the shaft, the scrotum, or the rectum manually at the same time, and the shock value of the ice, together with the contrast of the familiar and reassuring warmth of the hand, is, well, mind-blowing.

Other things that are stimulating in the mouth for oral sex are marshmallows, which are soft and squishy-squashy; toothpaste, which tingles; and fruits, which are juicy and tasty and exciting for both lovers during tandem oral sex, or sixty-nine. She can chew a banana in her mouth while sucking him, or have one in her vagina while he eats her as well as the delicious fruit. Crushed strawberries are erotic elegance, too. However, my all-time favorite fruit for sexual encounters is the peach.

The peach reminds the man of the woman's vagina, because it is fleshy and juicy. On a warm summer night you can chill a firm, ripe peach and share the nonforbidden fruit. You cut in in halves, remove the stone, and each lover takes a half. He rubs his pulpy piece on the woman's vagina to give it a succulent taste when he eats her out, and she uses the other half to do the same to his penis, which makes it squashy and delicious.

When a man sucks or kisses a woman's vagina, especially her clitoris, the clit tends to get an erection that's like a penis in miniature and very exciting to him when he feels the little knob grow in his mouth. For a man, when the clit grows against his tongue, it means he is doing a good job of sucking her, and he is getting a response that will trigger off vibes to his penis and give him a big hard-on. I once had a call girl working for me in Manhattan who was the first woman I ever paid money to sleep with. Everyone who had sex with her raved about the experience.

This girl, Gwendoline, had no great looks to speak of, and, in fact, she was quite ordinary-looking, with lusterless reddish hair and too many freckles. What she did have, of course, was a big attraction. She had a trick clitoris that started like a small fingernail but would grow to the size of half my finger when it was sucked, and became virtually like a small-scale penis. The men were so crazy about it that whenever they came back they especially requested to fuck Gwendoline.

All things in moderation, however. I know of a man who once slept with a hermaphrodite, a woman who had a complete vagina and also a tiny but complete penis. And he was terribly turned off by that. So too much is not too good.

I know quite a few men who get really discouraged if they can't find the clitoris—when it is either too tiny, really hidden away in the folds of the vulva, or they are too clumsy to locate it. Sometimes even authorities on sex are the victims of old wives' tales. One of them told me that the position of highest clitoral sensation in any particular woman moves about "from hour to hour," and so a man should not be too harsh on himself if he cannot locate it. Experience tells me that this is simply not true. I have never encountered a roving clitoris, and I've seen my share and more. However, on different women it *is* located in different positions. A man cannot assume that because one woman was turned on by the position of his finger or tongue work in a certain place, the next woman will have conniptions in response to exactly the same procedure in the same place.

Proper clitoris stimulation is an art in itself, and a lot of men never seem to master it. There are no written rules—only, literally, word of mouth. But a step in the right direction is to gently probe around with finger or tongue, and never, never use heavy pressure, because there are hundreds, if not thousands, of sensitive nerve endings concentrated there, and only a cast-iron clit could stand it.

Let the woman indicate what is exciting her most. I don't get turned on when a man puts his hand on my clitoris before I am yet aroused. I don't like him to start with manual stimulation first. However, I get very turned on after oral stimulation, after there is saliva there from his giving me head. Then I sometimes take his hand and guide it in circles around the clitoris, never directly on it.

A lot of men do not know that right after the majority of women have an orgasm the clitoris reacts like a penis and you can feel it pulsing, almost imperceptibly, up and down. That is why, if a woman wants to lie to her lover, there is nothing easier than faking an orgasm, because he does not know of this postorgasmic pulsing in her clit unless his tongue is very sophisticated.

The easiest way for a man to perform oral sex on a woman is for her to be on her back while he lies with his head between her legs and spreads them so they wrap around his shoulders. This, of course, is a solitary sucking position and would not work if they both wanted to participate in oral activity.

There are few people who don't care for sixty-nine because they prefer to concentrate the pleasurable sensations on one partner at a time. This is personal preference, but speaking for myself, I love sixty-nine. To me it is an exciting treat to divert his penis from my mouth to my breast while he is eating me. I lie on my right side, say, and nudge and nuzzle his penis against my left nipple, which is lubricated all over by some sweet-smelling body lotion so the action won't dry up. This way I can reach an orgasm almost instantly, much quicker than by sucking him, because the erogenous zone around the nipple sends electric vibrations down to the vagina while he's eating me. Even if his eating is not so good—if he's beating around the bush and doesn't quite hit the clitoris—just the stimulation of that exciting penis against my nipple will send me right off. There are probably sixty-nine different ways to enjoy *soixante-neuf* if the lovers have a fertile imagination and a desire to excite, which can be the most provocative accessory to the act.

A carelessly—or even deliberately—left-on article of clothing or jewelry can be mind-snapping to more men than most women realize—the strand of "respectable" pearls that crackle and tangle against her breast or around his hard penis as she sucks him. Sultry Asian women always knew the value of erotic ornamentation. Bracelets jangling up and down the wrist can suggest a penis in a vagina, or letting the bracelets brush playfully over his cock can be especially exciting. Elegant silk scarves that stay cool against the flesh of his penis or her breasts are a tremendous turn-on.

Those "furtive fifties" gloves, long, black, and slinky, that women wore in the pages of the porn publications of that era are a great "stroke" of erotic imagination. If he is the leather-loving, garter-gazing, whore-fantasizing kind of male, garter belts and corsets are good props, although probably more often used for fucking than sucking. Quite a few men still believe in that oldish "lady-in-the-living-room, whore-in-the-bedroom" adage, and even the most conservative men like a fantasy-fulfilling brush with whorishness.

I had a girl who called herself Tinsel and who used to turn up for work in my luxury penthouse brothel dressed like the cheapest kind of street hooker. She wore the hottest hotpants, and makeup that looked as if it was applied with a combine harvester—three layers of eyelashes, and hair so teased you could have lost your way in it. I advised her, "Tame it down, please." So instead of three sets of eyelashes, she would wear two. But the customers loved her, and she used to blow more guys than anyone else. Even after work she would still look like an explosion in a paint factory, but she had a boyfriend who also really dug the way she dressed, and he was so proud of her that he would take her straight home and fuck the pants off her.

Sweaters (and nothing else) on either partner can be quite a turn-on. I recently asked my lover to stay in his sweater while I went down on him, and its manly smell and the idea of his wearing it really turned us both on. All the clothes left on, once in a while, is exciting if she spontaneously opens his fly when they are in the living room and not yet in the bedroom and gives him a blowjob. Another thing that is a turn-on is a woman dressed only in vivid lipstick.

The sight of glossy scarlet lips around a naked penis is very exciting to many men. So is a pair of hands with long crimson, vicious-looking fingernails.

Although the possibilities for an exciting blowjob are limitless, there's always the man who can never be satisfied. Just recently, one of my male friends told me he never gets off from a blowjob during a sexual encounter with a girl in a bed, no matter how luscious she is, even though she might be the best cocksucker around. Even if he's eating her silly, he still can't reach orgasm. However, the moment he's driving his car in the heaviest traffic, or parking it in a crowded lot where there are people walking back and forth, he gets an immediate hard-on and a burning desire to have his cock sucked, preferably with his pants all the way down. And in his fantasy, the only way he can reach an orgasm is by pretending there is some kind of an audience around him.

This man, it turned out, was not just a Walter Mitty; he did actually fulfill his way-out fantasy when he persuaded a girlfriend to go down on him when they were sitting in the car. It was the end of a workday and still broad daylight, and as the girl sucked him, he peeked through closed eyelids and saw people, particularly women, staring in amazement. But he didn't acknowledge them until he realized his life's thrill and had an orgasm in the girl's mouth in front of everyone.

Unfortunately, there is still the occasional oral dilemma that can't be solved. A recent one I came across was the wife with the mouth too small for her husband's large penis. "I've got to please him orally, otherwise he might get it elsewhere," the wife wrote.

"There is no solution to that," I replied, "so I advise you to just work around the problem."

CHAPTER THREE

Masturbation: I. A Handbook

I once knew a man whose idea of foreplay was to lie alongside me and masturbate himself. One night I got up on my elbow and asked him in exasperation where he got his greatest kicks—from sex with his wife, sex with me, or from masturbating.

The son-of-a-bitch had the gall to answer, "Masturbating—because that way I meet a better class of people."

While he was not one hundred percent right, he was certainly not all wrong. Contrary to folklore, superstition, and jokes, masturbation, or the gentle art of self-stimulation, is not the secret perversion of the sexually unbalanced and will definitely not grow green hairs on the palms of your hands.

Far from it. "Masturbation does no harm at all," Kinsey said when he disclosed as far back as 1958 in his famous report that ninety-two percent of American men enjoyed doing it. Of the remaining eight percent, some, he said, had abnormally low sex drives and the others, I would guess, were probably too shy to tell the truth.

Because of the current sexual candor, the letters I receive, plus my extensive first-hand experience, indicate that that figure is now several points higher. I think all men—and most women—have masturbated at one time. Every kid of fourteen, fifteen, or sixteen, when he wakes up with a hard-on, will know that he has to do it.

Masturbation is evolutionary and natural and is to sexual maturity what talking is to conversation. Recently I was giving a lecture to a college audience in a remote district of Canada and a good-looking young man raised his hand and asked, "Ms. Hollander, when are you going to open a brothel out this way?" "Why should I," was my reply, "when I am making much more money vertically than I ever did horizontally?" "Because," was his frank answer in front of his friends, "I am getting sick and tired of going steady with my right hand."

Done guiltlessly and without shame, masturbation is one of the best specific sexual exercises for men and women. With those women who do not even know where their clitoris is situated, let alone know the feel of an orgasm, it helps them discover both. The male can train himself to withhold ejaculation, to slow down and to give his lover a chance. I know men who, in anticipation of a date with a lovely girl, will masturbate frequently, wondering whether or not she will go to bed and what it would be like. It stimulates the man's fantasies. And if the girl does say yes when they finally date, he doesn't ejaculate prematurely in his anxiety to have her—in his fantasies he's already done it.

Masturbation has other benefits. Some doctors say regular ejaculation is a physical necessity in the adult male to drain off the five to thirty drops of seminal fluid manufactured hourly, which, if unrelieved, can cause congestive prostatitis. It also aids what I call "absentee impotency." The penis has a memory that has to be exercised, and if unused in times of long separations, divorce, or widower-hood, it forgets how to function in some situations. Masturbation is a handy *aide-memoire*. Masturbation also beats pregnancy, rape, incest, and adultery. And it's legal.

This business of "absentee impotency" is not to be taken lightly. A merchant seaman was once sent to me, suffering from this very problem of absentee impotency. He'd just returned from a three-month voyage on an oil tanker where he'd had no access to women. Because of a strict upbringing, he couldn't bring himself to relieve himself by masturbation, and for three months he had rigorously repressed all sexual feelings. Once ashore, he had tried intercourse with four different women and each time had failed to make it. By the time he reached me, he and his penis were thoroughly estranged and out of sync. I understood immediately what was wrong, and began a gradual and careful "reeducation" of his penis, starting with very gentle strokings and suckings. On our second session, he was able to have an erection, and I had him get inside me, but didn't pressure him to perform. At our third session, he had a rip-roaring good orgasm, and his penis "graduated" *summa cum laude*. I sent the sailor away with a brief, to-the-point lecture on the absolute necessity of masturbation to tide him over the lean times.

Masturbation starts in earliest infancy, when a baby, feeling the pleasurable warmth of its urine, becomes aware of the sensual reaction of an erogenous zone. It continues with young children when they discover the erotic rewards of specific manipulation, and continues in healthy and adjusted individuals to some degree throughout their lives. It is well known that mothers in primitive African cultures take advantage of this childish pleasure and use it as a pacifier. In certain wealthy families, even to this day, the old servant uses it as job insurance as she addicts her little charge to stimulation of the anus. If and when she is fired, the child is restive and unhappy until the parents reinstate her.

Once a man complained to me that when a woman satisfied herself sexually it was called "self-gratification," but when a man did it, they called it "self-abuse." This, he said, was a clear case of sex discrimination. But whatever it is called—onanism, auto-manipulation, self-stimulation, stropping off, jerking off, beating off, jacking off, beating the meat, pocket billiards, pulling the wire, polishing, or, as the English call it, wanking—it's a pleasure.

Psychiatrists define masturbation as any form of tactile stimulation whatsoever, done habitually to give a person sensual pleasure. That means you could be masturbating at this moment, as you are reading this book. If you are constantly twisting a lock of your hair, thumb-sucking, repeatedly playing with a favored finger, or rocking gently back and forth as you sit in your chair, you are, technically speaking, masturbating.

I have a compulsive "masturbating" habit of inserting my index finger into my left ear, no matter where I am or who is around, and wiggling it like crazy at a tremendous speed, and I just can't stop until there is a little "pop!" accompanied by a feeling of sensual relief. The ear is an erogenous zone, and this "pop" goes right through to my groin, and in a small way I feel as if I've just come.

Masturbation is not just a solitary act; many times it is a mutual one. Done between lovers, it can be a very exciting prelude to, or variation in, lovemaking. I love to lie with my lover, side-by-side or belly-to-belly—it is quite essential that you touch bodies or hands—and masturbate him while he masturbates me. However, it is a bit difficult to reach an orgasm at the same time. What turns people on during mutual masturbation, quite often, is the sound of the heavy breathing when they feel they are reaching orgasm.

But for all its pleasures and psychosexual benefits, there is still a lot of shame, guilt, and embarrassment attached to masturbation. In some penal institutes, to this day, an inmate can be punished if he is caught masturbating. I have heard that there are, even now, mental institutions where a patient who masturbates is isolated and sometimes put in a restraining device of some kind. It was not too long ago that mentally deficient members of a community were held up as tragic examples of the results of masturbation. In these cases, completely turning cause and effect around, it seemed to the pious and prim that the fact that the crazies played with themselves was evidence that masturbation led to mental derangement.

Also, until quite recently, the United States Naval Academy at Annapolis ruled that a candidate would be rejected by the examining surgeon if there was evidence of masturbation—which would more than likely mean putting the whole fleet into boxing gloves, or mothballs! The Boy Scouts manual through 1945 spelled out the perils of pulling, and narrow-minded members of the medical profession endorsed this quaint notion. They predicted everything from pimples, digestive upsets, insomnia, fallen arches, dandruff, blindness, neurasthenia, genital cancer, insanity, and sometimes even death.

But nobody ever died from masturbation, except Onan, son of Judah, in the Book of Genesis, and his fate was punishment from the Lord for having lain with his brother's wife. Anxious to avoid "issue from his act," Onan the adulterer "spilled his seed upon the ground," giving the name "onanism" to the practice of masturbation.

And nobody ever went crazy from masturbation, either. Quite the reverse. Kinsey accurately called it a normal and natural sexual outlet, which alleviated nervous tensions and helped people lead more balanced lives.

If masturbation can be so worthwhile, where did it get such a bad reputation? In most cases it was condemned on religious grounds, especially in the Catholic and Orthodox Jewish faiths, which disallow, as a perversion and a sin, any sexual activity that promises no chance of resulting in reproduction. Recently, on a radio panel program in Quebec, a predominantly Catholic community in Canada, I talked with a radio announcer after the show. He told me that during his twelve years of marriage, during which he and his wife had practiced the rhythm method of birth control, he had had sex with his wife only two or three times each month, whenever the calendar would allow. The rest of the time, he said, he would have gone mad if he had not given himself sexual relief through masturbating. However, because of his religious background, he spent most of the time feeling guilty about it, and the rest of the time in church confessing about it. He even felt better for confessing to the Happy Hooker!

Parents, inhibited by their own generation's sexual secrecy, unaccustomed to observing sexual behavior of any kind, embarrassed by their own sexuality, have also encouraged an unnatural feeling of shame and guilt over masturbation. There's no clinical evidence of masturbation disturbing a child's adjustment except when adults have either reprimanded or punished him or, worst of all, threatened to amputate his most precious possession, the penis. A mixed-up Jewish youth once came to me because, when he was a boy, his parents had intruded on every part of his personal life, supervising all his bathroom and bedroom habits, including masturbation. He was a typical Portnoy kid, and he told me he had discovered a way, through masturbating, to get even not only with his meddling and sexually suffocating parents but also with the whole world.

He had no chance to masturbate, even in his own room, where, the moment he closed the door, his father would ask, "What's going on?" But he found a kinky way, finally, to masturbate. At night, when the family was safely asleep, he would take a globe of the world from his bookshelf and remove the metal bracket to expose a hole (which he enlarged adequately) at the North and South poles. Then he would insert an insulating wad of Kleenex into the hole at the North Pole before he buried the whole thing snugly into his pillow and got revenge on his parents by fucking the whole world. Obviously, this youngster is no distant relative of Philip Roth's Portnoy, who found a cored apple irresistibly seductive, and who even violated a piece of liver behind a billboard on his way to a bar-mitzvah lesson. Of course, all this occurred when he was much younger than in the WASP fellatio incident previously mentioned.

I certainly don't deny that there are dangers to masturbation that may require psychiatric therapy or marriage counseling. Some men can't ejaculate inside a woman and have to finish themselves off by masturbating. My first boyfriend ran into this problem, and it was mainly my fault. I refused to let him come inside me out of fear of pregnancy (and utter ignorance of contraception). He'd make love to me and give me an orgasm, get out of me, and then masturbate until he came. After a while this became his sexual pattern and he became incapable of having an orgasm inside a woman. I had made him into an onanist, and it was quite frustrating to both of us. Such cases, unfortunately, aren't too rare, and the only excuse for them is sheer ignorance.

In some marriages, if one or the other partner continues to practice masturbation to the point that it indicates a lack of partner adjustment, it can be devastating to the future of the relationship. However, a lot of women I know say this is the only way they can reach orgasm. I used to resent my partner's masturbating and say, "Am I not good enough?" But now I know that if I go along with his occasional wish to masturbate, it can be quite exciting for both of us.

Obviously, when masturbation is practiced as a solitary form of sexual release, to the exclusion of partners, there is a problem. This can be a case of narcissistic or fetishist preference, an activity conceived in loneliness and one that only keeps reinforcing itself.

Another biblical masturbator, a lady this time, was also punished by the wrath of a disapproving God. In Ezekiel 16:17 she made "images of men and didst commit whoredom with them." How she would have loved a twentieth-century vibrator!

If masturbation is practiced to excess, it may be damaging, although to this day none of the experts have been able to give a satisfactory definition of the word "excess." Masters and Johnson conducted a survey with 312 masturbators and asked each one his opinion of "excess." To a man, each said it had to be a level higher than that in which he indulged. A man who did it once a month said he thought once a week might be too much. A man who masturbated three times a week felt six times a week to be excessive, and so on. However, Kinsey had one respondent in his famous report who confessed to a twenty-three-times-a-week habit, with no apparent adverse effects.

Although the human race may believe masturbation is their invention, that's not so. Animals—birds, deer, dogs, elephants, and porcupines (who may not have much of an alternative!)—do it. Even dolphins masturbate by placing the erect penis, which is very versatile because it is also prehensile and can grasp things, into the jet of a water intake in their aquarium.

Of course, humans, I've discovered, are even more resourceful in their methods of masturbation. I've known men who masturbate by inserting the erect penis into such objects as a half grapefruit, a whole orange, a folded pillow held in place by a plastic trash bag, between pillows on a bed, or the flat hand and a mattress, or trapping the penis between the thighs and rocking the body. One young man wrote me that he got very turned on to his mother's Hoover, but I don't recommend it, since the foreskin, especially in an uncircumcised penis, can get painfully sucked into the tube.

A nineteen-year-old once wrote to me that, whenever he gets excited after looking at girlie magazines or some girl on the street, he goes and finds a place to masturbate. However, he likes to use a nylon stocking or pantyhose, his sister's or mother's bra, or any part of a woman's clothing to hold in one hand while he masturbates with the other. Sometimes he masturbates in the stocking or in the pair of underpanties. He would meanwhile fantasize about making it, for example, with an older neighbor of about thirty-five who lived next door and often sat out in the garden. While he masturbated he looked at her suntanned body in her bikini.

Another man is an inmate at a federal reformatory, where there are no women with whom the men can satisfy their needs—only some so-called "queens." He, however, prefers to masturbate in a sock, size 8½, with a lubricant inside, preferably Alberto VO5 shampoo. He can control the point of climax up to one and a half hours.

Another friend of mine, a homosexual, likes to masturbate with a picture of a male nude in one hand. He then closes his eyes and visualizes the body of the person in the picture, or of his favorite idol or lover, only sometimes the face. He then says out loud words like, "Suck me, fuck me, touch me, kiss me," while he masturbates. He also likes to masturbate in the following way: he buys a French rubber and fills it up with hot water like a balloon. Then he puts a pillow underneath his stomach and holds with one hand the filled-up rubber around the penis so he gets a warm feeling as if he were really fucking someone. He finds the sight of his growing penis, optically enlarged by the water, quite exciting.

Some people use artificial vaginas, inflatable dolls with a vagina and real hair, made of rubber that feels like human flesh. I even heard a story that, on one naval ship, the men had a female doll painted around a hole in a wall; when this contraption was to be put to use, a little faggot was bent with his ass against it on the other side. This, of course, was hardly conventional masturbation. You might call it masturbuggeration.

Atmosphere is very important to many men who like to masturbate. For example, they enjoy lying face-down on a beach, where the balmy combination of sun and gorgeous girls in bikinis turns them on. And we've all heard about the man, usually older, with the masturbation guilt complex, who puts his soiled raincoat across his lap in explicit sex movies, and the other kind who brings his binoculars to the strip-tease, even though he has a seat in the front row.

I heard of another dirty-old-masturbator who always picked a seat in the movies beside a young boy, and when the lights went down, inserted his penis through a hole in the bottom of an open box of candies and invited the boy to help himself. Some like to rub up against men or women in crowded subways, which is called *frottage* and is illegal.

A doctor friend of mine told me he was forever being asked to remove objects, such as hairpins and ball-point pens, from the meatus—the eye of the penis—and from the rear end of men. Other things they use in anal masturbation include candles, carrots, cucumbers, Coke bottles, unpeeled bananas, dildos. This is probably a made-up story, but I was told that a man even lost his vibrator and it whirred away inside him until the battery wore out! Some men and women train a pet to lick them to ejaculation, but one man complained that dogs don't have the attention span to finish the act. Also their tongues are kind of rough.

Larry, who was my boyfriend for a few years, once gave me a beagle for Christmas. As a reward to him I taught the dog to lick his penis, which I must say he enjoyed at the time.

I'm sure there are lots of boys who masturbate over pictures in *Playboy* and *Penthouse,* and another popular helping hand is the massage-parlor girl, especially rampant in Los Angeles, where with the aid of some body lotion it's a one-two-three deal.

Still others love the slow, erotic teasing of nature's inventions, like, as one man wrote to me, fucking a slender white field lily. Water is another helpmate, and a strong, well-directed jet, played continuously onto the penis in the shower, is a favorite with many men. Masturbating with water is a favorite of mine also, and I like to lie in the bath with my legs spread up against the wall and my clitoris exposed to the steady warm flow from the faucet. However, there are not too many places outside America where this can be done, because hot and cold are usually from different spigots in other countries and can't easily be mixed to a comfortable temperature.

Recently I discovered another great bathroom turn-on, quite by accident, when I placed my electric toothbrush on the edge of my washbasin while I inspected my teeth. The appliance was switched on and merrily vibrating; the basin happened to be crotch-high, and I had a fantastic orgasm there and then.

Just as each person has a favorite masturbatory aid, so there is a preference in technique. It has been established through clinical observation that the differences are length, strength, and stroke.

One man might grip his penis with a tension that would give another man a headache, or cockache, and another may hold his so lightly that it would tickle another man to distraction. One might concentrate his attention on the glans alone, pulling at it with only his fingertips, although this is very unusual. In uncircumcised men, the glans is rarely exposed during masturbation, unlike in intercourse.

Usually, however, most men generally duplicate the experience, as nearly as possible, of actually being inside a vagina. And although there are different strokes for different folks, there is, in fact, a standard or classic method of masturbation. Nearly all men hold the shaft of their penis with the strength of a snug vagina, develop a regular beat back and forth, barely touching up against the corona, or rim, of the glans, speeding up significantly as ejaculation starts to build. Then they either clutch their cock spastically on the paradise stroke, or, as many men do during sex as they plunge their penis as deeply as possible into the vagina, stop moving and let it relax and trickle or spurt out.

In partner masturbation there are standard golden oldies too. I get very turned on if my lover takes himself in hand and masturbates against my breasts, interchanging with sucking them, which makes everything nice and moist. He is actually fucking my tits, either in the cleavage while I hold them together, or against my nipples; this is especially erotic because it is an erogenous zone for a woman and it goes right to her brain. This is what a lot of women should suggest with their lovers instead of making the excuse that they don't want sex because they are having their period.

There are many variations on masturbation for that time of the month or for when they want to do something different. She can masturbate him, he can do it to himself, or they can put body lotion between the cheeks of her ass and he can masturbate into this voluptuous cleavage as she kneels or lies on her stomach. The body lotion is useful for masturbating men who are circumcised, as they tend to get very dry. She can also combine stroking the shaft with oral sex, by licking the tongue around that knot where he is circumcised and allowing the juices from her mouth to run down all over the whole shaft.

Most people have masochistic moments to some degree, and the following is an exciting way to masturbate at such times. She ties him down, wrists and ankles, so that he cannot under any circumstances put his hands on himself or his partner. His cock is erect and exposed and trembling to fuck, but that is the one thing he cannot be allowed to do, because a masochist's greatest pleasure is not fucking but being teased—in other words, suffering. She can let him eat her pussy, or even put her cunt around his penis for the briefest tantalizing moment, then take it away. When he is going crazy, she can eventually jerk him off, or free one of his hands and let him do it to himself while she does it to herself.

A less elaborate way of getting a man excited, particularly if he's tired after his first orgasm, is to knead the penis between the hands as though you're making dough, or to roll it between your palms like a Boy Scout swiveling a dry stick to start a fire.

In the next chapter I'd like to turn to a subject that has seldom been openly discussed until recently, except in textbooks—the sexual fantasy. While it is common to fantasize another person, such as a favorite movie actor or actress, while having sex with one's companion, it is in solitary masturbation, where the partner is absent, that most people have their wildest fantasies, a kind of symphony to accompany their ecstasy. The secret dreams are usually of forbidden fruit, a wishful concept that, if by some remote chance it were ever fulfilled, would cause the fantasist to keel over. We'll soon see why.

CHAPTER FOUR

Masturbation: II.
Mit Fantasies

It's safe to say that no solo masturbation takes place without at least a bit of fantasizing. But here we're interested in the supercolossal variety, the kind that would make a Cecil B. De Mille blush. Psychiatrists find fantasies an illuminating glimpse into the psyche of their patients. And we laymen and laywomen can also learn a great deal from them.

From most men, through their letters and confessions to me—and this may surprise you, as it did me—I have discovered that if there is one pattern of preference running through the masturbatory fantasy world it is that of bestiality. Following is a typical example.

Two young women with long blond hair hanging loose over their naked bodies are riding along a beach on horseback, without saddle. They are both on the same horse, a stallion of course, and the girls are fondling each other and pressing their cunts against the horse's back as it runs along the surf with a tremendous, stiff hard-on. Then the girls dismount and start playing with the stallion's cock, while the masturbator by now is fantasizing that he himself is the horse and the huge penis the girls are caressing is his own. The horse transforms into half-man, half-beast, the male part of course being the dreamer himself, and the girls are his final goal. You might call this semibestial wishful thinking.

Another fantasy is a blueprint for the typical voyeur and performer. A man walks through the woods; it is summertime, and everything is green and pretty. All of a sudden he comes upon an opening in the thick bushes and sees a children's playground where three young girls, about twelve years old, are frolicking around and playing badminton. He comes closer and sits on a bench, watching as their short dresses fly up, revealing their white cotton undies. The girls are as he loves them, nice and almost boyish, with ribbons in their hair and lollipops in their hands. This really turns him on.

He wanders casually out of hiding and offers to play with them on the seesaw, where he sits in the middle, while on each side there is a young girl going up and down. He turns his head from side to side like a windshield wiper to stare up at the smooth young crotch of the up girl, while rubbing his own crotch against the undulating plank. He ejaculates on the spot. The slight variation is that he is squatting near the end of the slippery slide as the girls come down toward him, so that they will fall across his face when they land, their legs almost strangling him (in actuality he buries his face into his pillow to get the suffocating effect) and his tongue darting away in their hairless young virgin cunts while he meanwhile fingers their little clits.

For a change of pace, there is the wrestling or chastisement fantasy, in which the man gets turned on watching two fiery ladies go at it in a good old-fashioned row that develops into a wrestling match. He is sitting ringside, so close that he could even touch the two wrestlers, one of whom is strong and muscular, and dressed in a sexy tight corset with half-bra, her nipples sticking out and up, and wearing crotchless hotpants, revealing, with each kick at her opponent, a completely shaven pussy. The pinkish lips are inviting to his eager tongue but are frustratingly just too far for him to reach.

The other wears a red sleeveless sweatshirt with oversized armholes, and her perky nipples stick right through them; occasionally, when she moves her arms in a stranglehold or a forearm lock, one of the strawberry nipples pokes through. This makes the audience cheer wildly, and the fantasizer gets really turned on by the way the two fighting cats wrap their legs around each other's hips and waists, their tongues hanging out of their open mouths as they pant for breath, screaming in pain and yelling in anger. There's the counterattack, with fingernails, painted hot red, scratching really deep into the enemy's back, and the hands yanking out handfuls of hair. The masturbator is building up to the climax when the winning wrestler dumps the other to the canvas. While the referee is counting, for a finale she jabs her entire hand up her defeated opponent's open crotch and starts fist-fucking her.

The big-boob-lover's fantasy: he finds a huge South African black woman with a terrific fanny jutting out in back and a huge set of boobs up front, and his biggest pleasure is to imagine himself in a jockey's outfit riding her like a horse. She is on her hands and knees, and he spanks her big, firm bottom with a riding crop, all the while yelling, "Go, go, you fatass, run, run, you've got to win this derby!" Then he leans forward and grabs onto her mammoth mammaries while kicking her in her belly with his spurs. As they come down the stretch, he speeds up the beat of his wrist, and as they cross the wire, he comes.

The kidnapping is a typical masochist's masturbatory fantasy. He is walking out of a supermarket carrying a heavy bag brimming with groceries when two women wearing high black boots, the shortest leather dresses, and black masks approach him. They knock the bag to the ground, making the groceries tumble out and the milk spill all over the street. He is ordered to crouch down and lap it up like a dog before they dump the rest of the groceries and put the empty bag over his head. He is handcuffed and pushed into a long black car, with a girl sitting on either side. He is completely helpless and scared of their threats and rough orders, on the one hand, but also he is turned on by their lovely smell of sweet flowers.

After many hours of driving they arrive at a castle, where the bag is removed and he is thrown into a cellar with a medieval torture room and dozens of torture instruments. They strip him and hang him on a pole with his arms up in the air and his feet just a little above the ground and a pendulum hanging from his cock. Then the girls collect their girlfriends, and all of them start playing around with each other in front of him, all the while teasing him, with their leather gloves scratching at his balls, tweezing his nipples with their sharp nails, putting needles through his scrotum. The weight of the pendulum causes him great discomfort, but he digs the whole scene and is turned on. Then they bring a huge double dildo over, and one of the girls takes him off the pole, ties him on his hands and knees on a hard wooden board, and straps the double dildo around her waist. She climbs up behind him and starts fucking his ass, while the other end of the plastic penis deeply penetrates her cunt as she moves backward and forward.

They have removed the weights and tied all kinds of cords around the head of his cock. While the girls fuck him, one by one, another stands in front of the table and orders him to suck her cunt, but every time he gets close, she pulls back and he is unable to get free from his bonds and reach her. She finally gives in, and he starts eating her as he manages to rub his cock against the wooden board, and thus, while being beaten, punched, and yelled at, he comes in the midst of all the hullabaloo and sexual fireworks. Not only is this dreamer boy of ours a certified masochist, he is definitely not a premature ejaculator!

Last—and also first, because it is an adolescent masturbator's fantasy—is the bath. A thirteen-year-old virgin boy sees himself alone in the house with his lovely mother, an attractive brunette in her early thirties, while his father is away on a business trip. She is about to take a bath. He has connecting rooms with his parents and manages to peek through the door; he sees his mother having trouble opening her zipper to remove her dress. He nonchalantly walks into her room. She looks at him helplessly and asks him to unzip her dress. It is a long zipper that goes all the way down to her bottom, and she wears absolutely nothing underneath. Meanwhile, the water is running in the bathtub, and she is ready to step in, but she's still shy and covers the front of her body with a towel while the kid pretends to move out of the room. He picks up a newspaper his father has left there and sits on the edge of the bed, but he can see, through the partly open door, his mother's sensual body almost disappear in the bubble bath in the mirror reflection.

She calls out that she has forgotten to take some soap, and would he bring a new bar from her drawer. The kid by now is horny, with a huge hard-on protruding in his pants as he walks over with the soap bar. He offers to wash his mother's back, and the next thing he realizes is that he is washing more of her front than her back, soaping her bushy cunt while he sucks her tits, which he always remembered, since he was an infant, as having tasted so delicious. They are still round and firm, and the nipples are as big as cherries. Then her maternal instincts come out and she lovingly soaps his gangling young body all over. She pulls him on top of her, and the water makes the slim thirteen-year-old feel as though he is floating inside her warm vagina.

I hold no brief against fantasies. Anything that leads to sexual self-fulfillment is fine with me. I've always enjoyed my fantasies, and they've made me happier with my sexual life. (In fact, I suppose a typical day in *my* life could easily be a fantasy day in somebody else's.)

But, given the opportunity—and, Lord, am I ever!—I would rather use live ammunition than blank cartridges. Masturbating is fine in its place, but as the man said, once you've mastered the finger exercises, it's time to graduate to the piece.

CHAPTER FIVE

The Erector Set, OR, The Adolescent Penis

Andy was blond, blue-eyed, and one of my most devoted fans. At twelve years of age, he was also one of my youngest.

He would follow my daily activities in the newspapers (of a city which shall remain nameless to protect the no-longer-innocent) and turn up at all the store book-signing parties to see me. He stood no taller than my armpit, but he always tried to sneak in a snuggle against my body. Often I would hug him back, which resulted in some adults saying, "Look, *now* she's seducing twelve-year-old boys." I don't mind having the reputation of screwing every guy in town, but I have enough worries without having child-molesting charges against me.

However, I was flattered by his attention, which was like a grown man's. Andy lived in the suburbs and had to ride the train and subway to see me. With his leftover pocket money he would buy me chewing gum and candy. He somehow managed to get hold of the address of my apartment hotel and telephone number, and he introduced me to his mother and father over the phone. He had three brothers, between fourteen and twenty-one years of age, whom he wanted me to meet also.

"Are your brothers as nice-looking as you?" I asked him. He said they all looked pretty much alike, but the others, being older, were naturally taller. This excited me a little, because Andy was a very pretty boy and would one day become a handsome man, but he was still too young to do anything with. Even though the body was not yet ready for action, the spirit apparently was, as I found out one morning.

It was about ten o'clock, and I had just stepped out of the bath when there was a knock at my door. I was dressed only in a man's shirt, which I like to wear with just a couple of lower buttons done up, and my ass was barely covered. However, I thought it was the bellboy with the mail, and since I'd already screwed him, I didn't care too much about how I was dressed.

I opened the door, and there stood Andy with a box of candy in one hand and cookies in the other. With him was his fourteen-year-old brother, Michael. "We just dropped in to say hello," Andy said. So I invited them in.

Michael was a delightful creature, with Andy's big blue eyes, but more mature than his brother. He told me he had read my book, *The Happy Hooker*, and was looking forward to meeting me. He was looking me up and down with a child's face and a man's approval, and I got so excited my nipples were standing up through my shirt. "How would you like me to play some music?" I asked them. They thought the idea was just fine, so I said to Michael, "Why don't you choose some records?"

He was shorter than I, of course, and he was wearing those thin summertime pants. When he bent over the record player, I let my shirt fall open and pushed up behind him, with my pelvis against his rear end. And even though he was innocent, he instinctively knew how to respond. He put his hands behind him and grabbed me right on the snatch. At that point I was already wet.

Meanwhile, Andy was staring at us with big eyes. He was jealous because he wanted to show me off to his older brother, but he didn't want to donate me to him. I figured I'd better give him some attention, so I handed him some magazines to read, *Playboy* and *Penthouse*, and I said, "Why don't you sit here and read these? I have to discuss some things with your brother in private." The bedroom I took Michael into had no key to lock the door, and while the excitement of wondering whether or not Andy would come in was at first very stimulating, it soon became clear that Andy was going to be more of a nuisance than anything else.

Pretty soon Andy started banging on the door. "What are you doing in there? I'm going to tell my mother. I'm going to tell my father." So I gave the kid some money for a Coke. I also handed him a copy of *The Happy Hooker* and told him to go downstairs to the lobby and wait.

I was finally alone with young Michael, who sat on the edge of the bed shaking a little. On the one hand, he was quivering with anticipation of what was going to happen, because he never dreamed I would even give him a second look. But on the other hand he was afraid and told me I shouldn't do it to him. He was also worried that Andy would tell his parents. "Listen," I reassured him, "I'll take care of it with your father. After all, I can only do you good, and I won't do you any harm."

I thought: Okay, I might as well take care of him thoroughly. So I stripped open his shirt and took down his pants. He had such a childlike figure—a slight build, and no body hair except for a soft fuzz of pubic hair coming through. He also had an amazing rocklike hard-on. He admitted he had had erections before and had jerked off, but he thought he would be a virgin until he was nineteen. He never imagined he would get laid at fourteen.

At first I started kissing him on his mouth, but I didn't want to waste too much time with the preliminaries because I was very excited myself, and I just wanted him to fuck me. So I lay back on the bed with my legs dangling over the edge, but he didn't know what to do. I actually had to lift him up onto my body. He was so lightweight that it was almost like having a child on me. Even so, his penis was nice and thick and about five inches long. Since it probably had still not finished growing, it was evidently going to be quite impressive.

I told him, "Keep your legs together and just put it inside me and move it." So he put it in, but I finally had to move him rather than his moving himself. He did about six strokes, and, bang, he came, just like that. But while he was still coming, he bit into my shoulder and just about went wild. I came also, because I was so excited.

Then I washed him off. He was very shy and rolled

over on his stomach to conceal his penis. With his voice muffled in the pillow he said, "Was I any good? I bet I was lousy, because it was my first time."

I said, "No, you were very good, but next time *you've* got to take the initiative." So I took a little time and taught him where the erogenous zones were. I started kissing him all over. But, like most young boys, he was very ticklish. At the beginning, it takes a firmer touch, because those erogenous zones seem to develop only when they get older. When I kissed his nipples, he just started giggling, because it's almost physically unbearable at that age. Also, I wouldn't recommend to anybody to kiss a young boy underneath his balls, or suck his toes, because it just drives him crazy with silly laughter.

But what he did like was to get his ear and his back kissed, and of course his penis. I didn't get as far as teaching him anything about oral sex, but I definitely taught him how to suck my titties. First he grabbed them, then he squeezed them, then he sucked them so hard it hurt. I said, "No, no, go easy. Pretend that I'm sucking your penis and flicking my tongue around it. You do the same around my breast." And in no time he had it up again, and this time I made him be the leader, the domineering one. He lasted a bit longer, maybe fifteen strokes, but I didn't have an orgasm at all, because I was too involved in teaching him.

Then the phone rang from downstairs, and it was Andy wanting his brother. "We have to go to school now," he told him.

And that was the defloration of Andy's brother.

The case of Andy's brother was fun, but it wasn't one of my smoothest seduction scenes. First of all, he had turned up unexpectedly at my house. I wasn't prepared for the whole thing, and we were in too much of a hurry. Also, there was the mental distraction of knowing his brother was roaming around and might knock on the door at any moment. Nevertheless, it wasn't bad, and I feel pleased that his sex life got off to a well-adjusted start. After all, that first encounter can make or mar the man, and more often than not it sets the entire pattern of his future sexual life. I never saw Michael again, but somewhere, perhaps at this very moment, he is making some girl very happy that she is in bed with him. And I think I contributed to it. Sure, I know that seducing a fourteen-year-old sounds terribly naughty. But maybe it's our puritanical standards that are unhealthy, not my behavior.

Adolescence is the most crucial time, emotionally and physically, in the life of the male. It's like a long tunnel that he enters as a child and from which he emerges as a man. The encounters he has in transit will pretty much determine his lifelong sexual pattern. If he's a well-adjusted boy and his first experiences are healthy, he will almost certainly come out of it a normally functioning male with a healthy appetite for the opposite sex. If he has a personality weakness, he can still make it, with luck. But he could also develop, through unfortunate experience, into an inadequate lover or even drift off into perversion. He could become, for example, a peek freak, a flasher, a child molester, a sadist, a masochist, a foot fetishist, or a homosexual.

During adolescence the male undergoes dramatic

body changes. He suddenly grows taller, acquires pubic hair, undergoes voice changes, and owing to chemical changes in the endocrine system, he may develop a temporary case of acne.

Adolescence is literally the coming of age, because it is the time of first ejaculation. This doesn't mean first erection or orgasm, because a boy has been capable of these all along. A lot of male infants have their first erection immediately after birth and have them frequently from then on. They also experience the sensations of orgasm throughout their young life. However, the seminal and prostate systems do not function fully until adolescence, so the boy can't actually ejaculate.

The average age of onset of adolescence has been fixed at around thirteen and a half years, but it occurs anywhere between eleven and fifteen years, though occasionally earlier or later. During preadolescence, sexual development centers mainly around curiosity regarding genitals. This is the playing-doctor-and-nurse period, or you-show-me-yours-and-I'll-show-you-mine. The preadolescent male often experiences involuntary erection, and it can be a source of deep guilt and embarrassment. He can be stimulated by such nonsexual activities as sitting in class, friction with clothing, taking a shower, receiving punishment, fast rides in elevators or cars, skiing, bicycle riding, horseback riding, sitting in warm sand, or urinating.

Around the age of nine and a half, most preadolescents have experienced some homosexual awakening, conscious or unconscious. Whether the young man carries this over into adult sex depends on his emotional makeup and on whether the interest was merely childish and harmless or involved deeper feelings.

The young male, as I pointed out, starts his active sex life after his first ejaculation. However, what happens from there on in depends on opportunity and inspiration. Masturbation is usually the first outlet. I recently got this letter from a horny student who had just discovered the sex urge. He wrote:

> Dear Xaviera:
>
> I am a high-school student, and in my school there are eight periods in a day. Every period is forty-five minutes long, and every second period I have a temptation to jerk myself off in the washroom.
> All the guys follow me into the washroom and watch, but I can't help myself, so I do it in front of them. I always say, "It feels so good." They laugh, but I don't care, because I can't resist myself. Please help me, or I will wear myself out.
>
> Tony

Of course, he won't wear himself out, although it's a fact that nearly all men at some time or other foolishly worry about how many "comes" they have in them and if they will use them up too soon. Men are not handed a lifetime voucher for a specific number of orgasms. In fact, it has been discovered that a male's lifelong sex drive is determined by the age at which he reaches sexual adolescence. The sex life of the early bloomer is considerably more active throughout its entire course than that of the late-comer. Nevertheless, Tony could possibly become a confirmed masturbator, an exhibitionist, or even a homosexual, because the thrill he gets from demonstrating in front of a bunch of boys may become as important as the orgasm itself.

At the onset of adolescence the young boy is mostly concerned with the mechanics of sexual change. Toward the end it becomes "application," or, "Where do I put it?" All he knows is he's got to fuck. His sex urge is developed, but his self-confidence is not, and he is not yet aggressive. I was responsible for an extreme example of this shyness. Even with Xaviera doing a fantastic job on a nineteen-year-old boy whose cherry I popped, he didn't screw for a whole year afterward. He told me he was afraid that in all other encounters he would be a flop without me as his partner. This was obviously primarily my fault. When I'm wrong I'm wrong. Evidently I hadn't taught him how to take the initiative in a way that would build up his confidence.

There are many virgin boys of nineteen and twenty years of age who are very attractive, but when it comes to getting laid, they're somehow too shy to press the point or too gauche in the way they go about it. While "where to put it" comes naturally, "how to find where to put it" is more difficult. To give you an example, I was lecturing to a college crowd in Thunder Bay, which is a small community in Canada, and afterward a group of boys approached me about opening a brothel there. They felt that the girls were mostly a bunch of prick-teasers, despite their professed liberal attitudes. Some of them had been dating steady for several months but were getting nowhere. The girls kept promising, "Next month; I'm not on the pill yet," or making other excuses.

Meanwhile, the boys were coming home after a date with "blue balls," or "lover's nuts," or "stone ache"—a pain in the scrotum caused by unfulfilled arousal. "We're good enough to take them to movies, buy their hot dogs, hamburgers, and drinks," the boys complained, "but when it comes to getting laid, they won't come across."

Later, when I had dinner with the professors, I found out what the trouble was. The professors were balling the hell out of the girls, who were holding out on the boys. The girls figured they had a better chance of eventually landing a boy as a husband if they didn't give in. It was a small community, and even in these times, a reputation for promiscuity was a pretty serious matter.

I also talked to a group of the girls; they admitted that point but also said the boys were too inconsiderate in their approach, using such suave lines as "Come on, be a sport—let me fuck you." Not only that, but when one of the girls occasionally did go along, the boy was clumsy in his lovemaking, usually coming one-two-three, without a thought for his partner's pleasure. On this point, I advised each of the boys to have a practice orgasm before meeting his date for the night if he knew she was going to screw him, and to direct his thinking pattern to his date as he did it.

I discovered that out of a group of thirty girls, there were about five who would ball any of the guys. They were known as the school whores, or the Happy

Hookers of the college—which is really applying an unfair standard.

The thing is, a young man has got to get it off somehow. It has long been traditional for a father to take his son to his mistress to have his cherry popped. This kind of parental guidance is well intended, but if Dad picks the wrong woman it can have a disastrous effect on the boy's future. The cherry-popping has to be stage-managed psychologically as well as physically. In other words, the boy must have some feeling for the woman he is going to screw. It can be a very frustrating experience if, for instance, she is a dragon lady, or makes fun of the boy. It can turn him off women for a long time.

On the other hand, the youngster could be treated like the sons of a lawyer friend of mine who handed them over to me as a Hanukkah present. Both of his sons were cherries. They were Jewish boys, of course, and the way their father approached it was very intelligent. He did not say, "Here, I'm going to throw it at you hot." He told them, "You're going to get a nice Hanukkah present this year from Xaviera Hollander herself, and it's something you'll remember for the rest of your life." He prepared them for the cherry-popping a week in advance, and even asked me to speak with them over the phone beforehand to establish a rapport.

The boys were fifteen and seventeen, very virile-looking, strong, and well-built, but understandably a little shy. They had been overprotected by their mother and chaperoned everywhere. They had read books and magazines about sex, and recently they had been very restless around the house.

The Hanukkah cherry-popping episodes were both in the same afternoon, but not, of course, at the same time. The older boy was a bit more aggressive than his brother. He had a girlfriend and had kissed and necked, and he knew how to open my bra a little quicker than the younger one. The older one didn't need too much guidance once he got inside me. But I had to tell him to go easy and not just go pumping away, because he got very excited at first. The younger one was even more excited and more clumsy, but for all of us it was a delightful experience. I sometimes wonder if those boys, when they become good Jewish husbands, will give their wives an especially hot loving at Hanukkah time in honor of Xaviera!

While PG-rated cherry-popping is often helpful, parental guidance can, in certain circumstances, be overdone. That's putting it mildly in the case of a mother whose letter just about floored me when I read it:

Dear Xaviera:

The idea of introducing my son to sex has often intrigued me, so I decided to try it out with my seventeen-year-old. After about a month of subtle seduction—undressing in plain view with the door open, wearing see-through nightgowns in his presence, and so on, but with no results—I decided to become more aggressive.

One day, when just the two of us were at home, and he was taking a shower, I walked in completely nude and, without saying a word, joined him. The next twenty minutes were enjoyable and educational for both of us. He delighted in sucking my breasts, while I gave his surprisingly large cock rhythmic strokes until he came. In the past six months we have frolicked in the bed or shower about five times, all of them lighthearted and pleasant encounters.

He now has a girlfriend his own age. Our affair has ended, and I look upon the whole experience as the ultimate in sex education for my son. My question is, do you think I should repeat the instruction with my other, younger son, who will come of age in another year or so? I'd be more than happy to oblige.

Loving Mom

This is PG entertainment that, in my opinion, should be X-rated. Where there is a lack of other opportunities, incest is more likely to occur. Incest, being a taboo imposed by our society for various reasons, is a very controversial subject. Nevertheless, the taste of forbidden fruit is still very appetizing. Since incest can hardly ever be separated from "guilt feelings" occurring either at the moment of incest or several years later, I would not promote it as a family game. However, incest between brother-sister has increased greatly over the last ten years, while incest between father-daughter or mother-son occurs less often, for fear of hurting not only the child but also the other marriage partner.

Another letter I received, this one from a young man, said:

Dear Xaviera:

About a week ago my beautiful young sister borrowed ten dollars from me. Since she has no job, I realized she probably would never pay me back. But yesterday I got a knock on my bedroom door at about eleven P.M. It was my sister, who said if I wanted to get paid back I should come to her bedroom immediately.

When I came in, she was stark naked. She is seventeen, and I always wanted to see her gorgeous body, and now I was looking straight at it. She had nice firm tits and a really nice hairy cunt, with beautiful legs.

For half an hour I fucked the living hell out of her, and we both enjoyed it. For the first time I got to know what it felt like to run my fingers in a nice hairy pussy. I even got to butt-fuck her. But my real problem is, she wants me to do it every Friday night. I would love to do it, but I want to know if you think it is perfectly all right. It was quite a jump from masturbating once in a while to fucking my sister. But I love it so much.

Eager

Many brothers have sex relations with their sisters, although most times they don't really complete the act. They either get sucked off or else pull back at the end for fear of impregnating them. Ten years later such a person will write to me, "I have trouble reaching an orgasm with any woman, because when I was younger I used to ball my sister. But I never really came inside her, because I was afraid she would get pregnant with a mongoloid child." In many cases, from that time on, the man has never managed to relate to an adult woman completely, and his sex life remains disturbed.

The thing is, he's going to get it off somewhere, and there are many brother-and-sister relationships that go undetected for many years, because the parents just don't want to know about it. But parents can head off this kind of behavior by facing the fact that their son has got to do what comes naturally, and they'd be well advised to see that he meets girls outside the family with whom he can have his fun and games.

A couple of years ago a group of New York parents was interviewed by researchers on teen-age sex, and at that time, many disclosed that they had encouraged their youngsters to live together with their lovers openly under the family roof. They believed it was inevitable and had decided they would rather have it out in the open.

I believe parents should adopt the attitude of, "Okay, if you have girlfriends or boyfriends, bring them home. I want to get to know them." Not at twelve or thirteen, but at an age when they are a little more mature and responsible, they should just be left free. That doesn't necessarily mean, "Go use the bedroom." But don't chase them out of the house.

Another problem is that some parents are too naïve or just don't want to recognize the symptoms of their children's sex drive. The father with the two Hanukkah kids told me what had provoked him to send them to me for cherry-popping. They were nervous and edgy and started prowling around the house looking for something to do, getting uptight and then getting into mischief to work it off. The seventeen-year-old especially was driving his father crazy because he had a girlfriend who was teasing him all the time. He was already a man and was pissed off at her because he wanted to fuck. And the younger one was just starting to look through girlie magazines and was touchy and irritable. So that was a sensible father who saw the signals and acted on them.

If the parents know the score, they can send their children away on a vacation to mixed summer camps, where their activities are under supervision and whatever is going to happen, happens. In that environment, their leisure activity is usually organized, and the parents don't have to feel guilty, since, if the youngster does make it, the parents at least didn't set it up or give it the official seal of approval. But these days, for the most part, sixteen- and seventeen-year-olds are pretty mature. They go off to Europe with their friends, or they go hitchhiking, sleeping together in tents. Obviously the parents must know what's happening.

Despite all this, as I mentioned before, parents don't always want to know everything. You can be sure that, in the case I'm about to tell you, neither the student nor the teacher bothered telling their experience to the boy's parents; and the parents probably would pretend they hadn't heard it if they *were* told.

A young man wrote that he had received no sex education at home or from books and tried to get some at school. In so doing, he literally became "teacher's pet." He told me that he had written his teacher suggestive letters with lewd words. He signed the letters "Anonymous," but she figured out he had written them. He thought she was going to punish him, but instead, she said, "Let's go for a drive in my car and I'll show you all the things you wrote about."

When she parked the car in a secluded spot, she told him, "Now, you wrote 'cunt'—this is a cunt. And you wrote 'suck.' Now, this is sucking. And that's your cock."

The boy never, in his wildest fantasies, had expected that the teacher would do anything like that. Naturally, after the ride was over, she warned him not to tell anybody. And she was conscientious enough to continue the instructions on several subsequent occasions.

Maybe someday this will be standard procedure for adolescents, and right out in the open. High-school students are taught how to drive and care for an automobile, not only through charts and textbooks but also with practice in actual cars. Why not apply the same practical technique to sex instruction? The students would love it, and so would the teachers. But even more important, the youngsters would learn the fundamentals of a healthy sex life in the only way it can truly be learned—through practical experience.

CHAPTER SIX

Top Banana at the Orgy

Conundrum: What is it that never bothers to dress but is always the life of the party, that always stays but never comes?

Answer: The most popular prick at an orgy.

At group gropes, it's like Alice's restaurant, you can get anything you want, no matter what your taste. But contrary to popular notion, orgies are not usually the wild licentious affairs that most people imagine. Indeed, although Emily Post never applied herself to the problem, there are definite and recognized rules of orgy etiquette. After all, this *is* social intercourse—at its most liberal.

At any well-conducted orgy, as at any other social event, certain rules of behavior (penis protocol, if you will) apply. One of them is that you leave your hang-ups at home. You wouldn't attend a swing with a serious emotional or physical problem, any more than you would go dancing with a broken ankle. (The only welcome problem you could bring to an orgy would be satyriasis, which is the technical term for the inability to get it down.)

Being clean and attractive is important. Even the French, who are not known as the most fastidious people in the world, pay a lot of attention to hygiene at an orgy. The bathrooms are equipped with bidets and stacks of clean towels and are used as soon as a participant has finished having sex. You still smell the sweat and sperm—it's unavoidable, especially if it's a big orgy—but at least it's fresh and not something carried over from the previous fuck. Incidentally, in view of the nature of the affair, I've learned to my regret that a woman can't expect a lot of oral sex. A man never seems to mind screwing a woman who has just made it with a number of other men, but he generally won't give oral sex unless he's the first one to make it with her that evening.

Another important rule is that you come with a partner and leave with the same one. You don't go to an orgy or a swing so that you can collect or exchange telephone numbers and cheat behind your date's back. The rules of the game are, "Okay, you can ball my man or woman, but do it in front of me here, not some other time or place when I'm not in on the fun."

You can be choosy to an extent, but don't add insult to injury. If you reject somebody, do it politely. No one would say, "I don't want to fuck you, you've got droopy tits," or, "You've got a small cock." Nevertheless, some gauche newcomers can be pretty obvious about it. All you really have to say is, "Not just now, thanks, I've pretty well had it for a while." And after you've turned somebody down, you don't just jump right in and screw somebody else. You wait ten or fifteen minutes for politeness' sake. There's a certain amount of "courtesy fucking" (within limits) at an orgy, and one thing I learned when I went to a swing in St. Tropez was that if the host wants it, even if he is Quasimodo himself, you have to give him a polite fuck. In this case, I'd been a guest in his house for a while, and I was told, "You'd better screw the host, because he's had his eyes on you for days, and this is the opportunity to reciprocate for his hospitality."

Be sociable and don't monopolize one partner. Some people have no orgy manners whatsoever and are inconsiderate of others who have come there to enjoy themselves. One famous woman writer I know, who claims to be a true libertarian, once came to a big orgy, grabbed the sexiest-looking man there, and commandeered the best bedroom with the only bathroom attached. She locked the door and didn't emerge until the wee hours, when she called a taxi and left without a word. This is totally unacceptable behavior. At an orgy, you share everything—best beds, lovers ... and yourself. You don't stick with your own lover, husband, or wife (or anybody else's) all night.

One of the cardinal rules to bear in mind is that if you can't park your jealousies at the door, you're better off spending the evening at home with a good book. I mean, don't *ever* be jealous, because you'll get very uptight, and so will everyone else. One woman I know, who'd never had group sex before and just wasn't emotionally geared for it, came with her lover, who, unbeknownst to her, did a lot of swinging on the side. I found the woman quite attractive, and before the party was very old, I was eating her. I made her come, and she loved it. Then she was just about to screw a very handsome guy when she suddenly noticed her boyfriend flat on the floor with a woman sitting on top of him. He was obviously ready to come, making all those wild noises and screaming in passion. She jumped up and shouted, "How dare you! You never told me you could enjoy it that much with another woman!" She gave the poor guy a nasty kick and ran from the room crying. The point of all this is: if you can't stand the sweat, get out of the sauna.

I used to have a personal orgy rule I applied with my former boyfriend, Larry, and that was: save the last dance for me. In other words, "I don't mind how many women you screw, but let the last orgasm be inside me." It may seem a strange and even childish rule for a superliberated woman, but somehow I wanted that moment, which can be the nicest of all at an orgy, to be my own, for sentimental reasons. I realized, of course, I was taking quite a chance, and I must admit that often when the time came for the last lay, Larry didn't.

These days, I would never go to an orgy with the man I love. I would go with a friend or somebody I liked, but if I really loved a man (in my free-style fashion), I would say no. I can't stand to see him enjoying somebody else, because I always say to myself that as long as I please him and he pleases me more than anybody else, why does he need somebody else? On the other hand, I wouldn't mind if my man went on a business trip (to Timbuktu, for instance) and screwed a hooker or picked up a girl whose name he didn't know and whom he would never see again. But I still wouldn't want to watch him getting off his rocks.

Although an orgy is generally an unemotional situation, it can be a very unhappy one for some men and women who have fundamental problems. Of the hundreds of women who write to me for advice on the subject, there are many to whom I simply suggest they stay at home. Here's a fairly typical letter:

Dear Xaviera:

I've had several children, and my body is not the greatest. My breasts are sagging, I have stretch marks, and I'm a bit overweight. But my husband is still very virile and needs his sex, and somehow he doesn't get turned on to me. We have been to this swinging club, and I found that he got all the action he wanted, but I was kind of left out. Or if I did get screwed, I felt it was what they call a mercy fuck.

Left Out

With women like this, I advise them either to improve their bodies with diet and exercise—or even resort to cosmetic surgery (breasts, thighs, buttocks, face lift, or whatever)—or to stop swinging altogether. A woman in this situation, unless she can pull herself up by her pectorals, so to speak, is better off finding other satisfactions and letting her husband have his solo fling at an orgy from time to time.

On the other hand, the kind of person I would advise to go to a swing or an orgy is the one who writes:

Dear Xaviera:

After twelve years of marriage and two beautiful children, my wife and I still feel love and companionship for each other, but our sex life has become a little monotonous and neither of us gets a lift out of it anymore. We don't know what to do and were wondering if meeting up with some other couple in the same situation would help our relationship.

Willing to Swing

To this man I replied, "By all means, meet another couple or two and try a bit of swinging. Don't go to an orgy of twenty people, but start out in a small group." Quite often there's more intimacy and pleasure at small orgies, because everybody can do it in the same room, and you can all chat among yourselves in between. Big orgies are impersonal and sometimes—although it's a contradiction in terms—less "orgiastic." It's the difference between shopping in a small personal boutique, where you have a certain rapport, and a large department store, where, even though the selection is wider, they couldn't care less if you buy or walk out.

How and where do you find an orgy? In the big cities there are many underground papers with advertisements for group sex, but you take the chance of meeting a very creepy group—literally pigs in a poke. Taxi drivers can usually direct you to the erotic clubs where there are no professionals or hookers, but where the atmosphere is still very uninhibited.

A lot of aspiring swingers might be quite surprised

to know there's often a well-concealed orgy nest right in their own backyard, or at least in the general neighborhood. There's a tremendous amount of group sex going on in the upper-middle-class "bedroom towns" of America, and it's very possible that that nice couple you saw in the supermarket on Friday and waved to at church on Sunday swung their brains out on Saturday. How do you find out? Whether it's an exclusive little clique, some upper-middle-class types who are bored soft and have formed a discreet swap group, or just another liberated couple seeking a likeminded pair, there are some simple ways to ferret them out.

For example, you can invite an attractive couple that shows promise over for lunch, dinner, or drinks. Once you're relaxed or a little high on cocktails or perhaps a bit of grass and feeling less inhibited, you can direct the conversation toward sex. You can ask, "Have you seen *Deep Throat* yet?" or "Have you read *The Happy Hooker* or *The Joy of Sex*?" Ask their opinion on these swinging "classics," and the conversation might well take a ninety-degree turn to the horizontal.

There's also a more direct approach, and one must have a feel for the appropriate moment, plus a bit of nerve. The man casually puts his arm around the shoulder of the other man's wife and simply asks, "What are the chances of you and me making it tonight, sweetheart?" He'll get a reaction, all right. He might also get a mouthful of knuckles instead of nooky—but probably not.

Another, less brassy approach is for the husband to

remark, "You know, my wife and I have been pretty conventional when it comes to sex, but we've become lots more liberal lately. In fact, one of these days I even think I'd love to see my wife make it with another man." If your new friends don't blow the joint at that remark, you stand a good chance of their blowing something else.

I keep mentioning the husband, or boyfriend, as the one taking the initiative, because it's usually the man who turns the woman on to orgies, and not the reverse. Men are naturally inclined to be polygamous. A man will often start by reading ads in sex magazines, gradually converting his wife to the idea. More often than not, once initiated, she'll come around to liking it even more than he does. But it usually takes the man to get things going.

Incidentally, most amateurs think if they could only get invited to a nudist camp they'd have it made. I admit an orgy at a nudist camp almost sounds redundant, but strangely enough, these places tend to be pretty prim, at least to the naked eye. Often, however, there's something going on behind closed doors. Nudist camps, which are usually strict about promiscuous sex, often do have crazy little groups of four or five couples who swing to a fare-thee-well. However, they jealously protect their privacy and don't want anybody from the outside to know about them or to try to mix in. My advice is not to bother. Or form your own little naked coffee klatch, if that sort of thing appeals to you.

What do I think of orgies? For people with a strong sex drive, I think they're great. I also think they're great for people with a weak sex drive. Let me explain myself. If you're in the mood, all that moaning and groaning will enhance it. If you're not, the same stimulus will rev up your motor and get you going in high gear. For instance, if a man can't come quickly enough, and another couple plops down on the carpet next to him, with the woman carrying on in high C, that will trigger it for the slow-comer almost immediately.

Activity at an orgy can actually be "anorgasmic," that is, you can spend the entire evening without having one. It's nice, obviously, if you reach a climax, but it isn't necessary. Some people just go there to have a good time, but a lot of women I know—including myself—don't usually reach total orgasm. There are many times when I've been to an orgy where I liked the people but just wasn't turned on. That doesn't mean that the social intercourse, as well as the sexual, isn't pleasurable. You can still have quite an evening.

The best kind of home-town orgies are the spontaneous ones. It tends to be a drag if you say, "Okay, this week we meet at Tony and Leonora's, and next week we meet at Joan and Nestor's." To me, that's just the same as running a big whorehouse, but without the money. Not only that, but if boredom with your own spouse is your reason to start swinging in the first place, there's still the possibility of winding up where you started by getting bored with the same familiar five others. However, it's still bound to be a hell of a lot more exciting than going to a formal cocktail party where people are making superficial small talk or sitting around and playing gin rummy for a whole deadly evening.

If there's an orgy capital of the world today, it is France, where bars and elaborate private sex clubs in places like St. Tropez and Paris cater to the desires of swinging men and women—or permutations of either. And they do it with great style. Generally, swinging in France is more the indulgence of the privileged or upper classes. I remember one orgy, or *partouze*, where two hundred guests were sent engraved invitations and served fine champagne and caviar before the festival of the flesh began.

Orgies are actually more widespread in America, but here they are the sexual caviar of the suburbanite. Indeed, there's so much suburban swinging now that it's a culture all by itself, almost to the horizontal life of the American upper middle class what Arthur Murray's is to the vertical. In many ways, orgies in America are organized like the local Saturday-night dance, prearranged with the usual crowd, the same familiar faces (or, should I say, organs), some wallflowers, and some who never sit one out.

If everybody at an orgy is attractive, they'll all screw and get screwed. But just as there are great dancers, there are also great orgiasts. For example, the most popular penis is the "lucky stiff" that can screw everybody without going down, or else can immediately get up again, time after time. The most unpopular is the one that can't even rise once to the occasion, or the pencil case, or the fastest gun in the West—the unfortunate dong that is afflicted with premature ejaculation. The most popular woman is the one who throws reserve to the winds and screws everybody with nonstop gusto. This is especially true at swings in America, where an all-out sexually uninhibited woman is still a pleasant shock.

Rome is something of an exception to many of the customs that prevail in other cities. Needless to say, this ultrasophisticated metropolis is hardly lacking in a free-swinging sex life. But when I'm in Rome I usually get invitations to join just one couple for a threesome, that is, a man and wife or a man and his girlfriend. This is a *ménage à trois*, rather than group sex, where at least four participants are required, and usually there are many more. While the Roman male—married or single—enjoys having two women make it with him *or* with each other, he gets very upset over another man's making it with his woman. Call it male chauvinism or the proprietary instinct or what you will, there's something about the typical Italian male that makes it difficult for him to stand calmly by while another man is screwing his wife or sweetheart.

This is obviously a far cry from the original Roman orgies, which stemmed from women-only ceremonies, where priestesses would "initiate" other women at an *orgia* (a word originally meaning "secret rites"). From these it was only a hop, skip, and hump to the Roman equivalents of Sodom and Gomorrah—Saturnalia and Bacchanalia. Both were notorious festivals of depravity, gluttony, and perversion.

So obviously there's nothing new under the moon. In fact, the modern orgy sounds like a sedate affair in comparison with the ancient Roman sex binge. With our fairly well-defined rules of etiquette, one could appropriately characterize today's orgy as a "social occasion." For example, in swinging clubs in London and Paris you often can't get past the door without a partner. They don't want any voyeurs or freeloaders sneaking in just to look around or maybe screw a girl for free without donating one in return.

Many people who have never been to an orgy in their lives ask me what they can expect, and how they should handle it. They're surprised to learn that conversation at an orgy usually revolves around anything but sex. Of course, there's some shop talk during the fucking, such as "Take a look at that girl—is she well stacked!" or, "That guy over there can go for an hour, and he's so well hung, too." But right after they've finished and are just sitting around the sidelines relaxing with a cigarette, most people discuss whatever topics seem to be of general and mutual interest to them. Just like at any proper dinner party, your orgiasts talk about the kids, the house, the car, a new diet, or the soaring prices at the butcher shop.

At the bigger orgies—say, for fifty or sixty people—it's rather like a supermarket, where self-service is the order of the day and everybody picks out what he wants. Sometimes, too, someone gets what he least wants—VD. A Dutch swinging couple who are very close friends of mine told me they're always relieved several days after each orgy to confirm that they haven't picked up a dose. He happens to be one of those men who can keep a constant hard-on for hours, putting his cock in twenty girls and making them have a good time without coming himself. This is lots of fun, but it does increase the odds against him.

An orgy is a wonderful place for fantasy fulfillment. For example, I remember one orgy where a man with sadistic tendencies was satisfying a masochistic woman by beating her buttocks with his heavy leather belt until they were bright red. There was also an older woman wearing high white boots and lots of chains, running around looking for younger guys who wanted to be walked over. A foot fetishist was jerking off onto the left foot of a pretty young girl, while kissing and worshiping her right foot, and two very attractive and feminine-looking women were in a corner experimenting with the rites of Sappho, clearly for the first time. The funny thing is, although you often see two heterosexual women kissing and eating each other at group sex, you never see it with men. It's not that they don't want to, but they are too uptight to do it in public—unless it's an all-male swing.

As I pointed out before, most orgies are socially conventional, in an unconventional way. But there are exceptions to every rule, and some swingers say, "Long live the exceptions!" For these orgiasts, the lengths to which they can go are limited only by their imagination and resourcefulness. And if these qualities happen to be in short supply at any given moment, I'm happy to contribute this suggestion that I received in the mail:

Dear Xaviera:

Recently I went to an orgy with my husband and three other couples. We were all looking for a different and exciting experience, and we certainly found it.

When I arrived at the house where the orgy

was arranged, I was told to take off all my clothes and lie on my back on the coffee table. Two of the girls held my legs up in the air, while the other one took a basting syringe and filled up my vagina with partially set Jell-O. Then the fellows were called in and given straws with which they eagerly sucked the Jell-O out of me. While this was going on, the girls fondled my breasts.

My orgasms were fantastic, and I came like machine-gun fire. It was the same for the other girls, who found it just as exciting. I decided to pass this on to you to recommend to swinging couples who have become bored with the usual.

Flavor Craver

P.S. The fellows all said they liked cherry flavor best.

My own group-sex fantasy was the following little melodrama: have one guy lying on his back on the bed and another guy straddling his chest and getting sucked by the first one. Meanwhile, I'm sucking the cock of the first man while I'm getting fucked from behind by a guy who is himself getting socked from behind by another guy. This I fulfilled recently at a small orgy at my place. It was very exciting. It's hard to believe there were only five of us—there was so much going on in so many places!

I don't recommend this, however, for beginners. Start with one other couple and then gradually work your way up the orgy ladder. I must warn you, however, that by the time you get to where Xaviera was in the preceding paragraph, I'll be swinging from a completely different chandelier. But you can have lots and lots of fun trying to catch up to me!

CHAPTER SEVEN

The Sign of the Cock: Your Sexual Horoscope

I have often heard it said that men born under the celestial sign of Scorpio are the best lovers on Earth. And while this could be a rumor spread by Scorpio men, many women have told me this also. The astrological explanation is that men of this sign are ruled by Pluto, god of the mythological underworld, which influences deep sexual undercurrents and an intense, almost obsessive interest in making love. Added to that, the planetary physical characteristics of Scorpios endow them with the necessary equipment—strong muscular bodies and large powerful penises.

On the other hand, Taurus men could claim sexual supremacy too. They are ruled by the pleasure planet, Venus, which makes them the most sensual lovers of all.

While my life doesn't revolve around the zodiac, I know there are literally millions of people whose lives do, and I'm convinced there's a great deal to it. I have frequently noticed a marked relationship between the sexual equipment and technique of men and their signs. Incidentally, you'll have to take my word for it, because I promised not to use her name, but I worked out this whole chapter with a friend of mine who is

83

one of the most famous astrologers in America. I guess you could call it an "Astrocock Chart."

Since it takes two to tango, I've asked our astrology sexpert to add a sort of zodiacal compatibility analysis to each horoscope. One might call these analyses "Celestial Match-Ups." One might, but I call them "Match-the-Snatch."

Should a Taurus man make a beeline for a Capricorn woman? Or would a Scorpio woman be more his type? It's all in our stars—and all set forth in this chapter.

If you believe in astrology, this entire Astrocock Chart will guide you in your sexual self-evaluation and your compatibility evaluation. If you don't, you'd still better make careful notes, because as sure as you're sitting there reading this book, you're going to encounter more than one attractive member of the opposite sex who believes fervently in the sun signs. This chapter will at least guarantee conversational compatibility, and you know what that usually leads to.

ARIES, March 21 through April 20. Symbol, the ram. Men of this sign are ruled by Mars, the warrior planet. They usually have muscular, compact, and combat-ready bodies. The Aries man often has only a lance corporal of a penis, but it has the skills of a four-star general. In other words, he's an adept swordsman. Marlon Brando and Warren Beatty are both Aries men in good standing.

Aries is dynamic, magnetic, and a true strategist, with a direct approach to everything. This, not surprisingly, includes sex, which he sometimes tackles like the Inchon landing. Emotion, for him, is a bonus to an encounter or relationship, and he'd settle for the prize rather than the striving. He's in a hurry to achieve his goals. Delaying tactics, no matter how pleasurable, can really irritate him. Foreplay to him is a tedious demilitarized zone. He'd rather be down there in the trenches of the combat zone. He's patronizing to women, the male ego personified. When he's in good fighting form, he gives his wholehearted concentration to the exercise, which becomes as memorable as a military victory.

Although he'd never admit it, the Aries man is subject to intermittent impotence, invariably based on frustration in achieving some material or career objective. At these times, he tends to put the blame, unfairly, on his sex partner. He does not like aggressive women, but he enjoys a little resistance along the way so that he can storm the barricades, and he much prefers not only to initiate but also to control the action. He is rarely a masochist, but likes bites and scratches as battle scars. His major thrust, however, is toward climax, the arriving rather than the getting there, whatever means are used. He comes with an explosion like a twenty-one-gun salute, which to him is the symbol of conquest.

MATCH-THE-SNATCH. The Aries male enjoys subduing a Sagittarius female, who is likely to put up just enough barriers to stimulate his appetite for conquest. Once conquered, however, she is well able to match his stormy passions. Next in line for this man's sexual attention could be the Pisces woman, who adapts herself to whatever technique her man prefers.

TAURUS, April 21 through May 21. Symbol, the bull. Men of this sign are ruled by Venus, the planet of pleasure. Physically, the Taurean has a solid, well-built body; strong neck, shoulders, and back; and a sturdy penis, which he uses to the best advantage of all involved. While his "bull-like" symbolism is his physical strength, he is a lamb emotionally.

The Taurean is the original sensuous man. His entire body is an erogenous zone, highly responsive to all-over stimulation. He extracts every last ounce of sensual excitement before, during, and even after sex. He is a toucher—even in nonsexual situations—and likes to pat, stroke, and caress. He is naturally affectionate and physical, and his traits include endurance and patience; while he may start with the speed of a turtle, he finishes with the thrust of a bull. He is easygoing and slow to give in to outbursts of emotion, but, once provoked or stimulated, he whips up a storm. This characteristic, expressed sexually, means hours of pleasure for his partner before he reaches his own stormy climax. His penis is slow to ejaculate and should not be rushed, but both partners can enjoy urging it on. He is equally content with a woman who wants multiple orgasms or with one who paces herself to his deliberate and deep build-up.

The Taurus sex drive is constant and is unaffected by other conditions in his life. However, he does tend to establish sex patterns and preferences early and can be somewhat inflexible about when, where, and how he makes love. This reliability factor can also make him a faithful lover. His romantic blind spot is his appetite—literally. Music is not the food of love for him, but a big hearty meal is. He likes to eat before or after he makes love, and sometimes both. Fortunately, I've never encountered a Taurean who likes food *instead*, and I doubt that one exists. Taurus man is almost invariably a safe and satisfying partner. Gary Cooper and Orson Welles are examples of Taurus men.

MATCH-THE-SNATCH. The Taurus man has a natural affinity for the Scorpio female, and together they can trigger a sexual earthquake. His sensuality will also be appreciated—and matched—by a Cancer female. He could easily spend the rest of his life with either of these zodiacal types, preferably in bed!

GEMINI, May 22 through June 21. Symbol, the twins. Men of this sign are ruled by Mercury, which gives them a strongly intellectual bias. Physically, they tend to be tall and long-limbed, and that includes the "limb" located in the area of the groin.

The Gemini man is a communications expert. He doesn't have sex in silence, but continually talks erotically or sometimes even laughs lightheartedly. Grim intensity is not part of his makeup, and he brings his breezy attitude into all facets of his life, including sex. He is essentially a cerebral rather than a physical type, and his body would rather respond to mental stimulation of a sexual nature, such as porno movies and books and sexy talk. He has brains, wit, and curiosity and is extremely experimental. He's the man for the woman who thinks she's had everything. A bedtime adventure—be it in a tent, aboard a helicopter, suspended from a chandelier, or whatever else appeals to him at the time—will be an eye (or leg) opener.

He likes to be titillated, intrigued, and fascinated;

he might be a trifle masochistic, and sometimes even bisexual He's rather high-strung, and when he's a bit overcome by nervous tension, that makes him less than the perfect lover. When he gets in that state, however, he can usually be beguiled out of it through the power of suggestion. Examples of Gemini men are John F. Kennedy, Bob Dylan, and Ian Fleming.

He dislikes overemotionalism and backs away from serious commitment. The woman he wants must be more than just a pretty face, and he doesn't enjoy sex too much with a noncommunicative woman. But a woman who gets across sexually provocative ideas can easily turn him on. The sign of Gemini rules the hands, which gives its disciples two more tools for erotic experimentation.

MATCH-THE-SNATCH. The Gemini man generally enjoys most of all a dynamic Aries woman, one whose instinct for sexual adventure can surpass even his own. Put the two of them together and they may well pack a lifetime of sexual derring-do into a relatively brief affair. Second choice for the Gemini male would be the Virgo female, but with this combination there would probably be a lot of analytical conversation—not that that's bad. They might even wind up writing a sex manual!

CANCER, June 22 through July 23. Symbol, the crab. Men of this sign are ruled by the Moon. Physically, he sometimes tends toward a moonish plumpness, with his penis proportionately fleshy—its diameter more impressive than its length.

Cancer is the maternal sign, and there's a noticeably strong link with the mother image. Don't get him wrong, though. He's thoroughly woman-oriented; it's just that in his relationships with women, he basks in maternal sunshine, or moonshine. Cancer is powerfully aroused by voluptuous breasts and likes to be babied, petted, and comforted. He's moody and emotional and prefers a sex partner he genuinely loves, as this gives him more of a sense of security (which he especially needs) than he derives from casual encounters. If his feelings are seriously injured or if he feels unappreciated, he can be impotent, and this makes him glum and brooding. But a female who can supply mothering traits can soon arouse him. Two famous Cancer men are James Cagney and Ingmar Bergman.

The Cancer man doesn't mind at all if his sex partner initiates the action; as a matter of fact, the passive roles and passive physical positions are more gratifying to him. This doesn't mean, though, that he can't hold his own (and hers as well) in the home stretch. He is sensuous and has erogenous concentrations in his breasts, back, and buttocks. He won't refuse a little chastising, spanking, or masturbation, mutual or solo, and loves lots of little baby kisses all over.

He is inclined to be a domestic animal and would rather be between the crisply laundered sheets in someone's well-kept apartment than anywhere else. The Moon, as it affects the tides, seasons, women's menstrual cycles, and other phenomena, also affects the Cancer's moods and desires. He is at his most sexual between the New and Full Moon periods, rather than during the lunar waning time.

MATCH-THE-SNATCH. The Taurus female wins the nod as the woman most likely to succeed in fulfilling the fantasies and desires of even the most oedipal

Cancer man. He would adore surrendering himself to every generous curve of her Rubens-esque body, and together they can produce enough sexual pleasure to satisfy a dozen less demonstrative types. A Pisces female would also please him enormously, not so much because of the specific matching of their temperaments as, on the contrary, because the zodiacal contrasts between the Cancer male and the Pisces woman make for a happy rough-and-tumble sexual relationship.

LEO, July 24 through August 23. Symbol, the lion. Men of this sign are ruled by the Sun, which gives them their magnetism, generosity, and general expansiveness. (Mick Jagger is a famous Leo, as were Napoleon and Cecil B. De Mille.) The Leo man usually has broad shoulders, slim hips, and is generously endowed—that is, well hung.

This is Leo the Lion, king of the bedroom, and anyone who ends up being screwed by him has a lot to be excited about. Who says so? He does, of course. The Leo man is very conscious of his beautiful body and big penis, and he has an ego to match. Whether or not his partner finds him one of the world's greatest lovers, he's already convinced of it. Leo is a flamboyant, very dramatic sign, and this man brings enough drama into the bedroom (or wherever) to fill an X-rated movie—with himself as the star, naturally. He likes glamour, dazzle, and luxury at all times, and is turned off by even remotely sleazy surroundings.

Leo believes he is just about the last word in the lexicon of sex, but the truth is that he can be quite inflexible when it comes to variety and experimentation.

Moreover, whatever he and his partner are doing, there is always the impression he's on top, whatever the actual position happens to be. There's his image and dignity to consider, and he has to feel he's the one in charge—and looking pretty spectacular, too. He likes to be caressed all over, kissed, and fondled, and if it is done in a worshipful way, he'll love it. In fairness it must be admitted that he does have a strong sex drive and can excel in receiving and giving pleasure, but not necessarily so much for his lover's sake as for the fact that it makes him feel like a terrific guy.

MATCH-THE-SNATCH. A Libra female is most likely to provide the kind of luxurious allure that the Leo man seeks, and her flattering admiration could inspire him sexually to outdistance even himself. Another tempting mate for Leo is the Scorpio woman, although one cautionary note must be sounded, for she can come up with a sexual challenge that may result in ecstasy or agony, depending on whether he can rise to the dare or must suffer the fall of valor.

VIRGO, August 24 through September 23. Symbol, the virgin. Men of this sign are ruled by Mercury. Physically they are usually slender, with a moderate-sized—and very neat and tidy—penis.

The Virgo man is Mr. Clean and Mr. Cool. He's reserved and undemonstrative, especially in public, and has a true dislike of calling attention to himself. This somehow gives the impression that there's not too much going in his sex drive, but he can also be Mr. Guess-Who's-Got-You! He's actually quite a horny guy, especially in his fantasies—which would surprise his friends—and the occasional fulfilling of them. Given the opportunity, he'll live them out with his lover, and he usually likes a good deal of variety in doing so, including some sado-masochism. However, whatever he does has a time, a place, and a preauditioned cast if possible. He likes sex behind closed doors, preferably in the conventional atmosphere of the bedroom. He is clean and fastidious, and the way he makes a dash for the bathroom after making love could give his partner pause; but it's just his nature and should not be taken personally. He doesn't take chances with his health—period. His calendar is very likely to be superorganized, like so: Mondays and Thursdays, gym; Tuesdays and Fridays, concerts or movies; Wednesdays and Saturdays, sex. Among the famous Virgo men are Leonard Bernstein and Charles Boyer; famous Virgos of the past include D. H. Lawrence and Lyndon Johnson.

Mercury makes him inquisitive and experimental about sex, a subject with which he probably became initially acquainted from reading rather than doing. But he still likes to know what to expect and where and when to expect it. His sex drive is relatively strong and constant, and though not overtly erotic, Virgo is aroused by provocative sexual images in books, films, and conversation. But there is something to this man's nature that makes him, at times, pull away from physical contact. This can be very confusing and disturbing to the lovers in his life, unless they understand that it is the nature of the beast and not a reflection on them in any way.

MATCH-THE-SNATCH. The Virgo male is well matched with the female Capricorn, whose general attitude toward sex is similar to his own. This includes a meticulous emphasis on before-sex and after-sex techniques, as well as the act itself. They are "how," "when," "where," and "why" people, who must organize even the most spontaneous occasion. As an alternative to the Capricorn woman, there might be more excitement for Virgo with the Sagittarius female, although her impetuousness could upset his balance, which might just be the best thing in the world for him.

LIBRA, September 24 through October 23. Symbol, the balance. Men of this sign are ruled by Venus. Physically they are usually very good-looking, with a well-proportioned body and a delicious penis. Marcello Mastroianni and George Gershwin were born under the sign of Libra.

The Libra man is the romantic of all time. He manages to create an aura of refinement, elegance, and charm wherever he goes, and this includes his sexual excursions. The planet Venus, with all her seductive charms, luxurious sensuality, and unending quest for the ultimate in pleasure, truly influences him. Libra much prefers an atmosphere of luxury and understated good taste in which to make love. In fact, if the surroundings lack harmony, are shabby, or otherwise offend his sensitivities, he can, like Leo, get quite turned off. He's the kind of man who turns up at a whorehouse with a bunch of roses for the madam. He has a taste for the bizarre, and often goes for the really far-out perversions, but he orchestrates it all like a great symphony, making it an experience of grace, charm, and romance.

He may think in terms of fundamental four-letter words, but he doesn't approve of actions expressed in these terms and will be disenchanted with women who are loud, uncouth, or too overbearing. He prefers the stimulating nuances of preparation for making love to jumping straight onto the mink-covered divan. Young or mature, the Libra man responds to the classic romantic environment—candlelight, soft music, a woman in a slinky black nightgown. Under this sort of spell he will pull all kinds of astonishing tricks out of his top hat with variety, subtlety, sensuality, and originality.

MATCH-THE-SNATCH. The Libra male can be strongly attracted to the lionesslike grace of the Leo female, to her outward indifference but deep-down smoldering sexual response. (This man enjoys subtly assaulting barriers; but no violence please!) An Aquarian female could also project that unique kind of sexual promise that magnetizes the Libra man.

SCORPIO, October 24 through November 22. Symbol, the scorpion. The sexual mystique of the Scorpio man is that his desires are eternally smoldering and just waiting to be aroused. Of all the types in the zodiac, he is the one who can see sexual symbolism in just about everything. Famous Scorpios include Richard Burton, Robert Kennedy, and Charles de Gaulle.

The Scorpio penis is a nymphomaniac's dream—it has a tremendous kick in its tail and can last for hours. The Scorpio man is sex incarnate. His penis leaves no avenue unexplored on its predestined collision course with the vagina. And when a woman has been screwed by it, she really knows she's been screwed. The Scorpio male tends to do whatever he is doing with all of his strength and dynamic energy, and, in fact, it takes a very sexy woman to keep up with him. However, he is somewhat overly intense about sex. What should occasionally be a lighthearted roll in the feathers can, to him, become the assault on San Juan Hill.

He uses his whole body in his sexual encounters; he's demanding, desires total response, and can make the earth rattle with his climax. Nine times out of ten, a woman should gratefully accept this as the expression of a basic and strong creative life force. (The tenth time, she should try to jolly him out of his overdedication to the worship of Priapus.) But while he can give the most demanding woman everything she wants, he can be a male chauvinist pig and treat her like a sex object. Of course, I'm not much of a feminist. My advice is to relax and enjoy it. Not so easy to live with is the fact that Scorpio is often inconsiderate and sometimes even sadistic, and if thwarted or deceived in his sexual expectations, he can be quite a tough customer. A woman ought to know her Scorpio lover pretty well before she tries any interesting tricks of her own. Perhaps she should insist on seeing his birth certificate just to make sure he's a true Scorpio. And then prepare for the worst—and the best.

MATCH-THE-SNATCH. The single-minded Scorpio male goes straight to the point; he spots his kind of woman with one intuitive and educated glance. The female he's most apt to score a bull's-eye with is the Taurean. The compatibility is mutual. For her part, she knows how to grab the Scorpion by the tail without even feeling the sting. And she never wastes any time getting to the point, either. A Capricorn girl, despite her somewhat aloof attitude, is another likely partner for Scorpio. The beginning of their affair might not be as impetuous or as torrid as with a Taurean, but their chances of winding up as long-term super-sex partners are actually better.

SAGITTARIUS, November 23 through December 21. Symbol, the archer. Men of this sign are ruled by Jupiter, planet of good fortune, good luck, and good times—and he has plenty of all these. He is usually tall, may become portly in maturity but doesn't give a damn, has a fine, serviceable penis, and enjoys using it. John Lindsay, Frank Sinatra, and David Merrick are famous Sagittarians.

This is the fun-and-games guy—good-natured, downright jolly as he matures, with the ability to enjoy sex, spontaneously and totally, as a harmless romp whenever and wherever it occurs. Sagittarius doesn't take it all too seriously but looks upon sex as one of life's many pleasures, to be tasted to its fullest, along with good food, drink, and other accessories to social intercourse. While he may not make a serious career of being a lover, he performs well under a variety of circumstances, and he does enjoy variety. For all his casual attitude, Sagittarius can be fiery and passionate, with a quick response to erotic stimulation. He tends to be impatient with too much foreplay but compensates for this by speedy recuperation. The Sagittarius penis is known as a "repeater." And who can complain about that?

The Sagittarian is generous, both with money and

with his assessment of others. He has expansive ideas and can easily see himself as a man with a devoted wife, terrific kids, and a gorgeous mistress, well able to support two establishments and keep both women sexually satisfied. He can drop in for a quickie before taking off on a tour and be equally enthusiastic over both trips around the world—sexual and geographical. The Sagittarian is the ideal lover for the woman who is willing to take him on his own terms. And the terms aren't bad at all!

MATCH-THE-SNATCH. The Sagittarian, with his generous spirit and friendliness, tends to look at all women through rose-colored glasses, to the extent that he even makes them feel they resemble his fantasy ideal—the *Playboy*-centerfold type. However, if pressed to decide on his long-term choice of partners, he is most likely to single out a lively and experimental Gemini female, or a vibrant and glamorous Leo.

CAPRICORN, December 22 through January 20. Symbol, the goat. Men of this sign are ruled by Saturn, planet of conscientious hard work and long-range plans. The Capricornian is usually lean and muscular, with a respectable-sized penis, which almost always performs on request. In other words, it rarely lets any of the three—it, him, or her—down. A good description of the Capricorn lover is that he's highly sexed but reserved. He tends to keep his sex life apart from his career, especially in his younger years, not establishing a status-type family situation until later, when he can afford it.

The trouble with the Capricornian is that you don't always know where you stand with this man. He has a way of keeping things to himself, and this can include his feelings for his partner, his reactions to their love-making, and even disclosures on the big secret as to when she can expect to see him again. It is usually certain, however, that he has made plans. He plans for everything he does in his life, and carefully works things out far in advance. (Richard Nixon is a famous Capricorn. Howard Hughes and Cary Grant are other examples.)

Capricorn has the ability to compartmentalize his life, shutting out what he considers nonessentials in favor of immediate priorities. Therefore, his sex activity may be erratic, as well as highly erotic, with periods of sexual feast, and famine when other interests come first.

When he is sexy, he is extremely so, but he can become temporarily impotent when major ambitions are frustrated, at which times he beats a retreat from the water bed. Because he's the sort who perfects his skills at anything he undertakes, he is a thorough lover, not too experimental or bizarre, but well able to satisfy the most demanding woman.

Saturn is also the planet of age, and Capricorn men, like good wine, improve with maturity.

MATCH-THE-SNATCH. This man is frequently attracted to his zodiacal opposite, the Cancer female, whose abundance of tender understanding balances out his caution and reserve. While she is most likely to be his preference for permanence, he could enjoy the excitement and challenge of a brief infatuation with an Aries woman. With an Aries, however, his desires lean most often to a mere wham-bam-thank-you-ma'am sort of affair.

AQUARIUS, January 21 through February 19. Symbol, the water bearer. Men of this sign are ruled by Uranus, the planet of geniuses, eccentrics, and other nonconformists. Paul Newman is a famous Aquarian, as were Clark Gable and Charles Lindbergh. Aquarians are usually physically attractive, with well-proportioned bodies. They also have a knack for making a little go a long way, for the Aquarian, it seems, was behind the door when large penises were handed out.

However, he is far from an ordinary lover, obeying as he does the natural laws of compensation. He is experimental, passionate, intense, sensuous, and romantic to the point that his companion assumes he is more interested than he really is. This may lead to her becoming presumptuously possessive. Because he is unpredictable, that sort of reaction may just drive him away. Nevertheless, those he loves and leaves usually tend to remember him fondly.

The Aquarian's lover can expect the unexpected, because with him it never rains but it pours. One week he wants nothing but to screw his brains out, then for the next few weeks or so he couldn't be less interested. He has a way of talking his lovers into all kinds of unconventional experiments, and also, though he is basically kind-hearted, a way of cutting a person dead with a detached indifference. He avoids planned assignations: give him the time, place, and person, and he may or may not follow through on it. Because of his unconventional personality and libido, the lover he wants at any given moment could be a woman or a man.

MATCH-THE-SNATCH. The Aquarian male loves

cerebral seduction—that is, erotically stimulating thoughts and images. Both the Libra female, with her natural sensuality and erotic ingenuity, and the Gemini woman, with her inventiveness, are adept at projecting this kind of magnetism. Whether this is followed up with intensity and sexuality, or becomes a platonic—but still fascinating—experience depends on her skill in handling his moods.

PISCES, February 20 through March 20. Symbol, the fishes. Men of this sign are ruled by Neptune, planet of poetry, music, art, and yearning for the unattainable. His physical attributes often incline toward fleshiness, but in a sexy kind of way. He has a nice penis that seems to have a probing, seeking, searching, irresistible life and character all its own.

He is regarded as the lover-boy of the zodiac, the true lover-partner, more generous sexually than the Scorpio, and there is little he will not do—sexually or materially—to give pleasure. His partner's pleasure is also his, and he thrives on it. He is romantic, emotional, affectionate, sensuous, passionate, and strongly responsive to sexual stimulation. He is very sensitive, erotically and erogenously, and his dream is to merge himself totally with his lover. He prefers sex acts that involve total closeness and mingling to those where kissing, touching, and caressing are beyond reach. He would hardly be a brothel's best customer.

Because of his deep emotional needs, the Piscean tends to feel insecure in his relationships and demands excesses of attention, affection, and reassurance. This is a creative man, highly impressionable, with fantasies (and he has a whole congressional library of them) that go beyond all bounds, due to his fertile imagination and susceptibility to love and sex. Harry Belafonte, Ted Kennedy, Rudolf Nureyev, and Rex Harrison are all Pisceans.

The Piscean could be the perfect permanent lover—if he were not so promiscuous. (Pisceans of both sexes find it very difficult to say no.) And because of his insatiable thirst for that which is beyond reach, he may never find the perfect partner. However, he will make a lot of lovers happy along the way.

MATCH-THE-SNATCH. The female most likely to succeed in calming the Piscean insecurity is the Virgo. She alone has the patience and understanding to apply herself to pleasing her lover—sexually and in all other ways. Pisces also finds himself excited by and attracted to Ms. Aquarius, but he may find her somewhat baffling. This can be the square-peg-in-a-round-hole situation, because no matter what she does to reassure him, the overload of sexual stimulation inherent in this combination, plus the Piscean's basic emotional uncertainty, may cause him to pack up his penis and go.

Astrology is the oldest of the sciences, if you agree that it is a science. And it is also closely linked to the most exciting branch of our scientific future—the exploration of the planets. Perhaps the insight it gives us into ourselves lies more in our minds than in our stars, but insight is the most valuable tool we have.

In this chapter, I suppose, unlike the rest of the book, we've been more concerned with your sexual know-*who* than your sexual know-how. But remember, the leading astrologers do not consider their art a fatalistic one. As they say, the stars incline but do not compel. If a man feels attracted to a woman who is not predestined for him by the stars, he can always determine his own destiny. There's only one last word on the subject—yours. In matters sexual, every man is master of his fate under his own special set of stars and under the one supreme sign—The Sign of the Cock.

CHAPTER EIGHT

Circumcision: The Kindest Cut of All

The first circumcision in Western civilization took place four thousand years ago when Abraham sliced off his own foreskin with a sharp stone.

That brave act became the symbol of Jewish unity, submission to God, and defiance of their tormentors. Painful though it must have been, circumcision was compulsory, and anyone who refused to submit would be "cast out of the circle of his people." The fact that the ritual is performed on a boy child on the seventh day after his birth makes submission a simple matter.

Today, many technical refinements later, and with more than ninety percent of American males being circumcised as a routine procedure, controversy still surrounds this "Band-Aid" operation. Some couples would swear on a stack of Old Testaments that circumcision improves sexual relations by making the permanently exposed head of the penis less sensitive during intercourse, thereby helping prevent premature ejaculation.

Others insist the exact opposite. They would mourn the loss of their precious prepuce on the theory that the exposed head becomes *more* sensitive and therefore ejaculatory control is diminished. Still a third group, uncircumcised men with normally functioning organs whom I have personally polled, say that because they are more protected, they are *more* sensitive and yet have more ejaculatory control.

"Phallic fantasy," sniff Masters and Johnson, who are well known for getting straight to the point when it comes to the penis. This famous team of sexual fundamentalists took two groups of thirty-five men—skinned and foreskinned—and conducted neurological tests on the surfaces of their penises for sensitivity. Their conclusion: there was "no clinically significant difference between the circumcised and the uncircumcised glans during these examinations."

I go along with this. The only evidence I've seen of any real difference is in uncircumcised young boys who have difficulty controlling their orgasms anyway, and they often pop their cookies in seconds. But as every man matures, circumcised or not, he develops his own level of control.

That sentimental sensualist Dr. Alex Comfort, the biologist who wrote *The Joy of Sex* and a card-carrying prepuce preferrer, says if you sacrifice your foreskin "there's a whole range of covered glans nuances you can't recapture." In his home country, England, Dr. Comfort may just be preaching to the converted, because that nation is unique in the English-speaking world for its diminishing circumcision statistics. In the 1940's, almost half of England's male population favored the operation. Today, a much smaller percentage of Englishmen are circumcised.

But even Dr. Comfort admits he knows of "no evidence for or against slowing down of sexual performance" in the circumcised-versus-uncircumcised males. He says also, and I don't agree, that circumcision makes no difference to masturbation, either. Maybe it doesn't to the man performing a solo, but I find it especially exciting to mutually masturbate with a man who still has a foreskin. I get an erotic bang out of rubbing the skin of the prepuce back over the head—it's so silky smooth to the touch.

I remember the very first time I saw a circumcised penis. It was when I was nineteen years old and I made love with a Jewish man in Holland. We didn't perform oral sex at that age, at least in those days and in that country, and I realized that there was a difference. The circumcised penis was very dry—or perhaps I wasn't turned on enough—but we definitely needed more lubrication.

And it's more difficult to masturbate a circumcised penis because of its dryness, as I've discovered from extensive first-hand experience. Often during the time I operated a high-class brothel in New York City, I would see an older circumcised man who had asked a girl to perform oral sex on him but who had some trouble coming. He would ask the girl to complete the act by masturbating him, and to do this he would usually ask for a lubricant, often Vaseline, which is kind of sticky (Nivea cream is nicer), to put on his penis so it was smoother and did not tend to chafe.

But a man who is uncircumcised doesn't need that. He has the skin, which produces natural lubrication. Against this is the question of appearance. The look of a penis is very important to a woman, and I simply don't get too turned on seeing a flaccid uncircumcised penis with the flabby foreskin hanging over it like an elephant's trunk. Very often, though, when an uncircumcised man gets an erection, it looks almost the same as a circumcised one. Considering mainly on aesthetics, I prefer to get involved with a man who is circumcised; after all, how long can a man keep an erection? And while mutual masturbation is more fun with an uncircumcised man, as I mentioned, masturbation still plays second fiddle to an honest-to-God fuck.

Going from hand to mouth, most professional girls I knew hated to perform fellatio on an uncircumcised man. They automatically knew they would have to drag the man into a bathroom if he hadn't already taken care of the matter himself. Sometimes a man would protest and say, "Hey, what is this, national checkup week?" But the girls would have to say, "Sorry, honey, but it's all part of the profession." This problem of hygiene is much less common, of course, with a circumcised man.

In fact, hygiene, to me, is one of the most important considerations of circumcision versus uncircumcision. I am a cleanliness nut, and I would never get into bed with a man unless I was scrupulously clean, and I like to see this trait in my partner, too. But I'm not always that lucky, as was the case in the Amsterdam affair.

I was visiting my family in Holland after I had lived in the States for a few years, where I had been mainly exposed to circumcised men—both Jewish and non-Jewish. While I was home, I didn't really feel like dating too many men, because Dutch people don't attract me; they're not especially romantic. However, I met a good-looking blond WASP-ish fellow and accepted his invitation to go pub-hopping.

Throughout the course of the afternoon and evening he drank a lot of beer, and I counted six trips to the bathroom. Then he finally suggested that we go back to his house. Since I knew we weren't there to discuss growing tulips, I slipped into the shower to freshen up. In Holland, the toilet is separated from the rest of the bathroom, so if you want to relieve yourself, you do it in one room that has only a small sink to wash your hands, not big enough to wash your whole body. Then, across the hall are the shower, bathtub, and wash basin.

So I bathed, and I expected my lover for the evening to do the same. But instead, he went to the toilet for the seventh time and went right to bed. I had asked him earlier if he was circumcised, and he had told me "Of course not." Most men are not circumcised in Holland, and he wasn't Jewish. There he was lying completely naked across the bed, and in the typically romantic Dutch way, he said, "Why don't you suck me off?"

I came close to him and kissed and hugged him and replied in the same subtle way, "Why don't you wash up?"

"I took a shower this morning," he said indignantly. He was really offended. Then I could see what I was going to be faced with, because I'd counted the times he'd gone to the bathroom and I knew he wasn't that clean. I virtually had to throw him into the bathtub and tell him to pull his foreskin back and drip-dry it afterward.

I had to say to him, "Look, honey, you've been to the bathroom seven times. I've lived in the States, and I know what it's like when a man is clean and when he isn't. I've also been a hooker, and one requirement I have is either wash it up thoroughly or take a bath and shower if you can."

But even though he reluctantly went and washed up, he didn't do it thoroughly. If you don't pull that foreskin all the way back and soap it up, there's still an odor, and it's really a turn-off. When a man showers, I shouldn't have to tell him, "Pull back your foreskin." I don't want to be too unromantic, but if I don't give him a lesson, he usually flunks the test.

Medically speaking, the battle between the circumcised and uncircumcised is running definitely in favor of the former. I've come across men who are not circumcised and have a tight foreskin that gets very chafed inside. Also, there can be inflammation under the foreskin that can involve the glans penis, or the head. This is known as balanitis.

There are men I know, however, who have not been circumcised but who do keep the skin pulled back at all times, which gives them the appearance of being circumcised. There's a way of doing it that seems to work with practice. I had a boyfriend who knew I liked his penis better when the skin was pulled back, so each time after he took a bath or went to the toilet, he would make sure he pulled the foreskin firmly back to rest behind the glans. After a few months he succeeded in training it to stay that way.

I've seen other men who have trained their foreskins to stay back as an alternative to circumcision, but I must say these men had fairly large heads on their penises. If a man has a small head in comparison to the shaft, then the skin is likely to slide back automatically to cover it. But if the head is thick and round like a mushroom, it's easier to keep the skin pulled back behind it.

There's another condition in which the prepuce is sometimes too long and the opening too small for it to be retracted, and it causes the man quite a bit of pain when he becomes excited. The medical name for this is phimosis, and I've heard that a very famous Hollywood star, known for his success with women, suffers from this physical irregularity. It may explain why he kept his clothes on during a sizzling and much-talked-about Parisian love scene in a controversial movie of a few years ago.

In this situation, doctors generally suggest circumcision, and I've known at least three men in their late twenties whose foreskin was too tough or too tight and had to be removed. In some cases, the foreskin will retract enough to let the head of the penis through, but it still forms a tight band behind the glans during erection. I've seen this cause the glans to become swollen so that the foreskin could not go back into the normal position when the erection subsided. In that uncomfortable situation, we applied a cold wet compress. I've since discovered that's what doctors advise you to do until the swelling goes away. The condition is called paraphimosis, and if it occurs, circumcision is usually prescribed by the doctor.

I've heard it argued that if nature meant man to be circumcised she would not have issued foreskins. However, you could say the same thing about the appendix and tonsils. No one really seems to know why they were handed out, and no one really misses them when they're gone. Sometimes the retaining of any of these three physical nonessentials can cause painful problems.

Research has established that cancer of the penis, which accounts for three percent of all cancer in men, is rarely if ever found in the circumcised male. In women, most doctors say that intercourse with an uncircumcised male makes cancer of the uterus more likely, probably due to smegma—the white-colored material consisting of skin cells mixed with secretion from the local glands—that collects under the foreskin.

There is not one known case of penis cancer found in a Jewish male circumcised at the beginning of his life. And it is not that nature has played an unfair game of racial roulette, either. Medical literature mentions cases of uncircumcised Jewish men—there are a few—developing penis cancer, and their wives being prone to cancer of the cervix.

No one is absolutely sure why the Jewish ritual of circumcision is performed on the seventh day after birth, but the reasons are more likely medical than spiritual. It is believed it has something to do with the level of prothrombin in the infant body. This substance, which is the blood-clotting factor, is more efficient after the seventh day. It is also said that separation of the mucous membrane and the glans is more difficult before the seventh day.

The practice of circumcision in the Jewish community is called *milah*, and the person who performs this ritual is called the *mohel* (plural: *mohelim*). In the days of the Talmud there was actually a Circumcision Street where these men operated, with the aid of the rather crude tools of their trade. Today *mohelim* have considerable training in their specialty and have refined their techniques and also their instruments, which are not conventional surgical items but their own inventions. In Mount Sinai Hospital in New York City, for example, the prospective *mohelim* attend a special school for eighteen months to study microbiology, hematology, psychiatry, and pediatrics.

So skilled is the rabbi-*mohel* with his small knife and metal shield that physicians often prefer his services to that of a surgeon when circumcision is to be performed. Queen Elizabeth of England, shortly after the birth of her first son, Crown Prince Charles, retained the services of Dr. Jacob Snowman, who is official *mohel* to the London Jewish community.

While in many places the circumcision performed in a hospital by a *mohel* is done according to strict local health codes—sterile surroundings and mandatory check before and after by a physician—the *mohel* is not infallible. Not long ago a woman and her newborn son were passing through Duluth, Minnesota, on their way to Los Angeles when the young mother suddenly realized that her infant was in the seventh day after his birth. She located a *mohel*, who not only removed the baby's foreskin but part of his little penis as well. Explaining apologetically that this was his first circumcision, the *mohel* quickly wrapped a bandage around the bleeding appendage and vanished. The baby was given over to the hands of a reputable plastic surgeon, who managed to remedy the error well enough for all practical purposes. Luckily, this sort of slip-up doesn't happen often, and luckier yet, in this case anyway, we're living in a period when medical know-how meant that the damage wasn't irreparable.

Though circumcision today is a matter-of-fact, routine procedure, in some primitive societies it has been the subject of some very bizarre rituals. In ancient Mexico, for example, on the twenty-eighth or twenty-ninth day after birth a child was presented to the temple, where high priests and their assistants placed it on a stone and cut off the prepuce. The severed foreskin was then roasted in the ashes of a ceremonial fire. And in some parts of Africa, the mother traditionally swallowed the cut-off foreskin, while in other areas the father loaded it into some kind of firearm and sent it soaring into the sky.

In civilized societies circumcision has met with a lot of resistance and is still not accepted in many modern countries. It became a fashionable topic for discussion in books and professional papers in the mid-1800's, but it was not until the early part of the twentieth century that the United States began to accept the practice. Now, together with Australia, America is the world's most circumcised nation. Canada's statistics are slightly lower, due to the French influence—in France a very small percentage of the male population has been circumcised. South Africa and New Zealand don't reject the practice, but most of their men (or their parents) still believe they can live without it. It has not gained popular acceptance in most European countries.

While circumcision is still basically a matter of personal preference in non-Jewish communities, from the standpoint of hygiene, aesthetics, and well-being, I personally believe that the circumcised penis wins over the uncircumcised—by at least a head!

CHAPTER NINE

Ten Ways to Pleasure the Penis, OR, Ladies, the Ball's in Your Court

In Malaysia, if you think you're losing your lover's interest, there's an easy remedy. You steal a pair of his shorts and a lock of his hair, borrow some money from his wallet, and then take them all along to the *bohmoh*, or magic man. He puts the money in his pocket, the personal effects in a big caldron, mumbles an incantation over the wicked brew, and—*mumbo-jumbo!*—all your problems are solved.

In Spanish Harlem you buy lotions and potions and weave a do-it-yourself spell until your lover feels renewed pangs of desire. In the rest of America, however, where one in every three marriages goes on the rocks (and at least half of the rocks are named Sexual Boredom), there is no simple abracadabra. Keeping your lover spellbound is entirely up to you.

The most celebrated *femmes fatales* of foreign cultures, such as the famous geishas of Japan, have practiced the delicate art of penis-pleasing through the centuries. In modern America, every good hooker and call girl knows the value of the erotic arts, and knows they depend on a fine blend of sensuality and sexuality—plus some very specific and carefully refined skills.

Whether you want to be a memorable one-nighter or the love of his life, there are certain "dos" you should cultivate. (Learn the "dos" and the "don'ts" will take care of themselves.) From my own personal experience as a lover, and my observations as a madam, I have compiled the Top Ten Penis-Pleasers.

1. THE HAPPY SNAPPER. I have heard it called various names—among many, many others, the honey pot, the private swimming pool, the pussy, the snatch, the cunt, and, of course, the vagina—but the most complimentary label of all for a woman's most cherished possession is the "snapper." A snapper is a vagina that its proud possessor can tighten at will. If it is well-trained, the woman who owns one will have few, if any, sexual anxieties.

Not surprisingly, the snapper is a woman's most important lovemaking accessory—both from her point of view and from her lover's. For her, it is her center of greatest sexual joy. For him, a snapper is the best of all penis-pleasers. Any man whose penis has been "milked" by a woman with a well-trained snapper will tell you there is no sensation to compare to it. In fact, there is a certain validity to the expression "rule by clit," and the woman with a good snapper can wield a surprising degree of power over a man. The next time someone asks, "What does he see in *her*?" think it over. It probably isn't anything he *sees* but something he *feels*.

Some women are fortunate enough to be born with a tight vagina, which they retain throughout their lives. (This is an excellent start, but they shouldn't rest on their laurels; a tight vagina is fine, but its owner still should learn what to do with it.) Others may not be so lucky, or may have lost muscle tone through childbirth, wear and tear, or just plain getting screwed by Old Father Time.

There are a few popular misconceptions about the mysteries of the vagina. One is that the vaginal barrel contains an intense concentration of nerve endings that make tactile stimulation mind-bending. This, in fact, is a myth. A woman's area of highest nerve sensitivity, as every sensualist knows, is the clitoris, and next to that, the entrance to the vagina.

Which brings up another big misconception. There's a popular belief that a woman who indulges in a lot of sexual activity must inevitably lose vaginal elasticity and therefore her adeptness in pleasing her man. This is not so. First of all, the average vagina, which is approximately four inches in length in a relaxed state, can easily accommodate the largest penis during coitus, not to mention a full-term baby during childbirth, and still return to its normal size. And speaking for myself, even though I worked as a prostitute for a few years and still, in my "retirement," enjoy sex as often as I can, I have a snapper that men say is almost as tight as a virgin's—and a hell of a lot more versatile.

In cabarets in Harlem, the girls used to pick money up off the tables with their snappers; in the Middle East they can lie still and jerk a man's penis off without either partner moving his or her body. And I have heard of girls in sex shows in Japan who can insert a peeled banana and disgorge it slice by snappered slice.

While few loving women will ever need to perform these freaky tricks, everyone wants a tight penis-pleasing snapper. Here's how to achieve it. Sit on a chair, insert a small object into the vagina—for example, a pencil, a ball-point pen (point retracted, natch), a carrot, or a tiny vibrator—and concentrate on holding it there. Direct your mind to contracting and expanding the muscles of your vagina to put pressure on the object. Keep all your other muscles still.

Next, stand with the object inside and walk around the room. If you're not sure whether you've located the right muscles, take a walk to the bathroom beforehand, start to pee, and then cut off the flow. This muscle sensation is the same one you feel while doing the snapper exercises. Do this a few times a day, perhaps ten contractions a session, and gradually, like all body muscles, it will condition into a well-toned instrument of pleasure.

It's a good idea to change the object from a smaller to a slightly larger one every now and then, just to make sure of the right isometric effect. Do these exercises around the house, sitting down, watching television, or standing at the sink, and I guarantee it will be one of the most rewarding domestic chores of all. Acquire this skill, and you'll see—or rather, your lover will feel—why I call it Penis-Pleaser Number One.

2. PRICKLESS PRICK-TEASERS. Foreplay, in my opinion, is as important as the actual fucking. A man who is a good lover knows that a woman is not as genitally oriented as he is and that she needs to be stimulated first at the various erogenous zones of her body, by mouth, tongue, and hand, which means kissing her breasts, neck, vagina, and other personal pleasure points.

For her part, even though most men are quite willing and eager to get straight down to brass tacks, she should take the initiative in delaying the action with some sensual preplay. She should explore his erogenous zones from top to toe. If the man is her husband or a lover of long standing, she may think she knows his most intense erogenous zones backward and forward, but I've discovered there are many neglected or overlooked areas for any man.

Let's not go into actual fellatio at this point. I covered that frisky subject from A to Z and back again in an earlier chapter, "Playing the Pink Piccolo." Besides, the idea here is to tease a man's prick without touching it. Once that has been accomplished, you can get down to cases. My purpose is to remind lovers that, just as foreplay works up to the sex act, there are exciting preliminary techniques of foreplay that work up to the big "O."

Just as the way to a man's heart is through his stomach, one excellent indirect way of teasing a man's prick and getting him very excited is by licking his navel; add a few little scrapes of the teeth for extra effect. After finishing with the naval zone, try a novel zone—never forget that novelty is the spice of sex life—the area behind his knees. A cluster of quick, light kisses will stir things up nicely, and the same goes for his shoulderblades. Suck his fingers one by one, his toes, ass, scrotum (gently), blow kisses in his ears, and lick and chew his earlobes.

As in all things sexual, however, a lover has to be careful; otherwise, it can be overdone. Even the experts make mistakes, as once happened with me. One afternoon a beautiful dark-haired college student came over to my apartment to interview me for his school magazine. He was well-built and had a naturally sensual face. He was a little shy and nervous, and obviously quite curious about the Happy Hooker. I decided to seduce him and suggested we both take turns freshening up. While he was in the bathroom, I turned down the covers of my king-size bed so we'd have the erotic atmosphere of the black satin sheets.

I was very turned on when he walked hesitantly out of the bathroom without any clothes—score one for the college boy!—and I asked him to come and lie face-down on the bed. I wanted to give him my deluxe foreplay treatment, so I started nibbling his ears, and then continued down his spine. (That's where the nerves are situated that send little electric shocks to a man's penis.) Soon I had worked my way down toward his ass. I was really excited at the idea of having his beautiful penis inside me, but that was not to be. As I inserted my index finger inside his anus to really turn him on, his body convulsed and he came all over my beautiful black satin sheets.

The moral? You can't tease the prick and have it too—not if you overdo it.

3. THE FUN BOX. Hanging on the wall of my apartment in Toronto is a picture of two horses standing in a field. One of the animals is just standing there looking into space, but the other one has something else on his mind. He has a penis the size of a loaf of French bread, and his forelegs are on the rump of the first horse, about to mount it. One of the reasons I keep this picture around is to test the reaction of my guests when they notice the fucking horses. Once in a

while someone will turn abruptly away and pretend not to see it, but more often than not I can see them either sneaking a look or frankly staring at it and getting excited by the image.

What does this have to do with pleasuring the penis? Well, sometimes you have to stimulate the mind before you can arouse the penis to the point where it is in a mood to be pleasured. Showing your lover pictures of sexual behavior—whether it's humans or horses—is like showing a good recipe book to the Galloping Gourmet: it gets the juices going. Most professional brothels keep collections of erotic pictures and literature on hand, and there's no reason why the private lover should not do likewise. This may surprise you, but the two themes most likely to succeed in turning on both men and women are these: women making it together and—surprise!—women and bestiality. Pictures of women with cats licking them, or dogs screwing them, are easy to buy at any erotic literature shop. There's also a Scandinavian series of a piglet that has a penis like a corkscrew, making it with a woman; this may sound really weird, but it's a tremendous fantasy turn-on. For more human-oriented but still offbeat tastes, pictures of women wrestling each other, women in black corsets and garter belts, and women masturbating alone are very stimulating.

Go out and get a small library of erotic literature to read with your lover while you're both sitting up in bed. Turn your bedroom into a private screening room and show an 8-mm stag film. You can pick them up at any rental place in a large community or order them by mail. For anyone who can afford it, there are videotapes that let you make your own horny home movies.

Keep a tape recorder around and make a recording of your lovemaking. That way you enjoy the same sex act twice. It's exciting when you record it, and stimulating all over again when you play it back. You can even play my record, *Xaviera*, specially created for lovers to fuck by. We're still working on his penis through his mind, right?

Another piece of equipment with sexual possibilities is the new SX-70 Polaroid, which makes instant and incredibly sharp color pictures. Of what? Why, of you swallowing his penis, of him eating your pussy, and of whatever else your imagination suggests. Lights are sex toys that should not be overlooked. Replace the white incandescent light in your bedroom with a colored light bulb; the best colors are green and red. Light some candles, but make sure they are the big, dark-colored ones that form deep wells of wax in the middle and cast shadowy images of you and your lover performing sexual acrobatics.

Sex-oriented articles of apparel may not appeal to the very straight lover, but the chances are that if he enjoys seeing you in garter belts, nippleless bras, crotchless panties, and whory baby-doll nightgowns, he'll go out and make the purchase himself. If necessary, plant the suggestion. Some men get as much pleasure from removing clothing as from seeing you wear it. Recently my boyfriend, in a fit of sexual impatience, actually ripped my nightgown to shreds, and this turned us both on tremendously. Since that episode, I have heard of an item that you don't need to destroy in order to get the same effect. It's called the "breakaway" nightgown, which he can tear from your body without actually shredding your expensive garment. I disapprove of this last item, however. You don't plan to be "raped," so you shouldn't dress for it.

Speaking of nightdresses: dress well or don't dress at all. While nudity may be the most natural condition for lovemaking, never underestimate the effect of a seductive or puritanical nightgown—one or the other. The classic long and slinky black nightdress is still a great turn-on, even though, to the liberated lover, it might seem dated or contrived. In another mood, or with another man, the frothy white pristine gown might excite his instincts for "having" a virgin. Whatever kind of nightgown you wear, make sure it's clean and fresh, and not torn, faded, or frayed. And get rid of that woolly flannel passion-killer—it may keep your body warm, but it will almost certainly turn him cold.

4. VERBAL INTERCOURSE. There are few things more discouraging to a man in bed than a woman who is a silent partner. If she just lies there like a stone and says nothing, how does he know if he's pleasing her? And if she doesn't verbally indicate, even if only with a moan or a groan—you can say a lot with just "Ohhh," "Ahhh," or "Mmmm"—that she is having a good time in bed, his ego will get squashed and he may lose his "lover's edge." After all, when you fail to respond to a man at a time like that, you're really failing to respond to his pride and joy, his penis. And our purpose is to pleasure and flatter the penis, not to dampen its spirits.

Every woman should, at times, be an actress in

bed. There are even occasions when she'll have to fake an orgasm for the sake of his ego. But if she overdoes it, he'll know; a man's sensitivities are at their sharpest at a time like that, and she'll damage the sincerity factor that makes their love life work. She should make her lover feel like a king, appeal to his ego, pay him compliments, even if the truth is sometimes stretched—but not to the breaking point. Every good hooker knows the value of a well-placed compliment. Originality is not the objective here. He'll be delighted with the tried-and-true, such as: "Honey, you're the greatest! . . . Give it to me—oh, I'm so horny for that beautiful big dick of yours! . . . I've been thinking about your cock all day."

It's incredible how thick you can lay it on without sounding phony or obviously insincere—and, in fact, without really *being* insincere, since there must be something about him that got you into bed in the first place. Remember, if he is not Robert Redford in bed and he knows it, talking as if he were can turn him off. After all, he's not deaf, dumb, and blind either. Nevertheless, everyone has something appealing about him. If size is not his big point, then tell him, "Honey, I love the way you use your tongue."

If he's doing something you don't enjoy, gently remind him to "Go a little easier on me" here or there. Then bolster it with, "I love the way you caress my breasts." Talk, but don't chatter. Breathe exciting words into his ears, like, "Fuck me, lick me, kiss me, hug me, give it to me, fill me with love juices from your stiff prick, don't stop, I'm coming!"

For variety, spin him a fantasy: "Wouldn't it be exciting if you and I were in bed with another beautiful young woman, and you licked her cunt while I pressed my vagina up against her tits?" Then, having planted the image, keep talking it up.

The main idea is that you can accomplish a lot with your tongue even when it *isn't* being expertly applied to the tip of his penis. Maybe I carry my fantasy too far, the one I've expressed throughout this book—that the penis has an identity of its own, as if it were the third guest at the love feast—but I sometimes think the penis can hear, see, taste, and smell as well as feel.

5. THE EROTIC ENVIRONMENTALIST. There's a saying from preliberated days that a woman should be "a lady in the living room and a whore in the bedroom." 'Tain't necessarily so. Apart from the fact that a good hooker often acts with abandon in the living room, where she is selling herself, and with soft submission in the bedroom, if that's what she senses the customer wants, the whole idea that there's a precise time and place for everything sexual is all wrong.

It's the unexpected about sex that keeps it so exciting. Changing the usual time and environment for making love is one of the most effective weapons for cutting off that great enemy, ennui, at the pass. It could be a spontaneous seduction in the living room, while sharing a drink or just talking about nothing in particular. Sometimes the woman should, out of the blue, start caressing him with all his clothes on and get him all excited. Then undo his pants and take out his penis and start kissing it and licking it. And when he gets tremendously turned on, both take off your clothes (or even leave them on) and fuck on the living-room rug.

I stress this point about surprise in this chapter on pleasuring the penis because, while a man's mind is sometimes slow to catch on to what's happening to his sexual sensibilities, his penis is apt to be several inches ahead of him. For example, a motion-picture executive once visited me in my apartment in Toronto, and he was all business, with his conventional dark gray suit and his briefcase tucked under his arm. I said to myself: I'll give Mr. Prim the surprise of his life, just to see how he reacts. I walked over and very formally shook hands with my right hand, but with my left hand I massaged his crotch rather vigorously. His jaw dropped a foot, and a bewildered expression came over his face, but his cock immediately and lustily responded to the treatment. In other words, his penis was smarter and quicker than his mind. (Later on, his mind caught up.)

Of course, a man is a stranger to you only once. But you can still take a husband or a lover by surprise if you show a little ingenuity. And vice versa. Recently, on my lover's birthday, he was opening presents, and we were sitting there playing with the blue budgie birds I had just given him. All of a sudden I felt very sentimental—and horny—and decided to pull his fly open, go down on him, and then take off his pants. As we lay there on the floor among the wrappings, ribbons, packages, and champagne glasses, the budgies chirped happily away. It was lots of fun, and mostly because of the element of surprise.

Another time, he had come to stay with me for a while, and because we knew we could always have a go at each other whenever we felt like it, the emotional side of our relationship had become more important than the physical side. Usually, before we lived together, whenever we stayed at his house we would make a point of fucking when we went to bed and when we got up; but on this Sunday morning we were content to skip it and shared a lazy, leisurely breakfast together. Then I decided to tidy up the apartment and began cleaning out a closet. I was in a shortie nightgown, and he was walking around naked, when he had a spontaneous urge to make love to me. At first I protested, "No, no, I have to finish cleaning out this closet." But he replied, "Forget about it and just hang in there." And while I hung onto the hangers, and became all wrapped up in the coats and dresses, he gave me a closet fuck, and it was an entirely different sex experience for both of us.

Obviously, in a household where there are children or other adults roaming around, you can't just screw on the spot, but this situation in itself can make the challenge of finding a different sex site more exciting. A recent American President, in need of sexual privacy, used to screw his mistress in the White House coat closet. (It was a roomy closet.) However, for a person with no public profile, it's much easier to take a hotel or motel room.

Motel rooms, because of their impersonal atmosphere, can be a very horny environmental adventure. Rent one, call up your lover or husband, and tell him to meet you at Motel X. Use some pretext or other; say you want him to meet an old school chum, or whatever. Try not to give away the game. Then, when he arrives, either meet him downstairs, like Mrs. Robinson in *The Graduate*, or leave a message for him to go to a certain room, where you are all perfumed and ready for seduction. Don't forget the drinks, and don't forget to draw the curtains.

When I was living in New York, my boyfriend and I were invited to a party in a New Jersey city that was quite some distance from Manhattan. Our hostess, a woman with a divine sense of sexuality, handed us a key at the end of the evening and said, "This is your love nest for tonight at the local hotel. Have fun!" We did—and to a great extent because of the unexpected rendezvous we tumbled into.

Couples who want variety in their sex lives but don't have the courage or desire to swap partners should swap apartments. Give a couple of friends the key to your apartment, then go home to theirs. Somebody said, "They do not change themselves who change their skies." Maybe not, but they sure lose their inhibitions. And that's the first step toward sexual liberation, and the ultimate in the pleasuring of the penis.

6. COMING TOGETHER—AND STAYING TOGETHER. Aim for mutual orgasm, but don't be disappointed if it doesn't happen every time. If it's a first-time sexual encounter, it quite probably won't happen, and not only that, the performance of one or the other partner may leave a little, or even a lot, to be desired. Most sexually sophisticated men and women realize that a new partner should be given a second, and generally a third, chance to shape up. Of course, if there's a basic lack of interest in the partner

as a person, or if you feel it's an exercise in futility or incompatibility, you may decide not to bother.

After you've both reached a crushing orgasm, try to prolong the closeness of the moment by holding and caressing. Afterplay is important to you both for a lingering and loving impression. Caress his penis, give it a pat, pay it a compliment—but without any thought of arousing it to action again. Continue your loving embrace for quite a while. Don't get up immediately and smoke a cigarette, or switch on a light, set the alarm, turn on the television news, or roll over and go to sleep.

And don't, on the other hand, coyly avoid telling him about anything that might have been a turn-off about his lovemaking. I personally am known to be very straightforward, and maybe too candid, if a man does something I don't like. For example, I'll often say, "Oh, take it easy, you're biting my clit," or "Slow down, you're banging my ovaries out." Generally, the relaxed euphoria after you've made love is the time to point out diplomatically and to correct for the future something that didn't please you. If it pinched when he nibbled your clit, tell him, "It feels nicer when you use the wet tip of your tongue instead of your teeth on my clitoris." Or, "You're so considerate and gentle, which is nice, but I can also take and enjoy rougher handling."

Some women make the mistake of coming up with an instant and automatic postmortem, such as, "Hey, wasn't that neat?" or, "There now, doesn't that feel better?" Don't talk like Florence Nightingale. If he wanted to screw his nurse, he'd pay a prostitute to dress up like one.

What does this have to do with pleasuring the penis? Plenty. Women hate it when a man acts as if she weren't there after he's had his orgasm. Why should a woman ignore a man's penis after it has nobly served her? The pleasure of afterplay may not be as exciting as foreplay or the actual sex act, but in a way, it has a deeper significance. Perhaps, however, this doesn't come under the heading of pleasuring the penis so much as pampering it. Both are important.

7. THE LOVE THAT BINDS. Many women, perhaps most, have a deep-seated fantasy desire to be sexually taken by force—in other words, to be raped. While I personally doubt that many well-adjusted women would want sex forced upon them by a stranger, I think most would enjoy being "raped" by their own lovers. It is very exciting for both the man and woman when he binds her hands and feet, blindfolds her, puts her on her knees and elbows, and comes from behind and fucks her. He can do it in different ways—forward, between her breasts, and under her armpits.

She should reverse things and "rape" him. She can put him in bondage, his wrists tied above his head and his ankles either fastened together or to the bedposts with his own neckties. They both know now that he can't fight back. All he has is that stiff cock. He can't touch or fondle her. She can tease him by holding her tits in front of his mouth; he'll try to reach her with his tongue, but she withdraws. Then she can just barely graze his cock with her tits, or even brush against it lightly—too lightly to generate any real friction—with her bush. It's like the tortures of Tantalus.

If he barely can't reach her, it will drive him crazy. If this isn't prick-teasing, and in a very exciting way, I don't know what is. After the tantalizing bit is over, if she has the right rhythm and movement, she can fuck him instead of his fucking her. He is entirely—and slightly masochistically—at her mercy.

For couples who feel bondage is sort of silly, there's another way they can have an exciting slave scene. She puts his hands under the pillow behind his head and orders him not to move. And there is a certain way of looking and demanding that sets up the slave atmosphere. Once more, he is forbidden to hold or touch her. She gets him to close his eyes and works on his fantasy world, building up tantalizing stories: "Now you're in a castle. You're being thrown into a big torture room with manacles and whips all around. They are about to release a cage full of hungry baby lions, who will come over and lick all around your big throbbing cock. . . ."

Even the most seemingly conventional people have masochistic moments, when the idea of bondage, torture, or discipline appeals to them. Strangely enough, the weather has a great influence. When I ran the brothel in New York, I could always expect a brisk slave trade on rainy or gloomy days. I've also observed that discipline is a big favorite with German and Italian men.

This is a story that some of my friends to this day find hard to believe, but it really happened in my brothel in Manhattan. I had a girl working for me whom we used to call the Fucking Wallenda because she had been raised in a rough and tumble circus atmosphere and had actually, at one time, been a tightrope walker. She was quite hefty and muscular and not really sophisticated enough for a high-class house, but she was excellent with slaves. Not only could she wrestle several rounds with any of them, but she could, if they were not terribly heavy customers, hoist them up on her shoulder with one arm and jerk them off with her free hand. She was a really nice person, and I don't know what became of her after she left me, but all I can hope is that, if they ever open a sex circus, Fucking Wallenda will be the all-purpose sideshow.

Straight lovers should test each other out, perhaps in a big warm bed when it's raining outside, to see if the mood is right for spanking or discipline. Or he might like to try a little gratifying wrestling. The most exciting way of doing this, in my opinion, is to cover the bed with a rubber sheet so that you can both roll around in a pool of baby lotion—naked. It's a hell of a lot more fun than trying to catch a greased pig!

8. TWO TO TANGO. The most morbid sexual experience I've ever personally encountered took place when I was on a promotion tour to a city in Canada. But don't get me wrong. It wasn't at all bad; in fact, I enjoyed it in a weirdo sort of way.

I was escorted to the television stations and bookstores by a prosperous businessman, who also happened to own one of the local funeral parlors. There was nothing unusual about him; he was married and had a couple of kids, and he had very nice manners. Around five o'clock he invited me back to the funeral home to take a look around the deserted casket-display area. He showed me all the different designs and qualities of coffins—different finishes, linings, colors—and I must say they were all kind of sensual. Then he selected one with cream-colored satin lining and ruffled pillows and asked me to climb into it. He wanted me to "lie very, very still, as though you're dead, and don't make a sound." And then he fucked me. It was a very narrow, tight fit, but quite exciting. Later he confessed to me he had actually committed necrophilia with two young women who had been brought in.

For the necrophiliac, screwing a woman who is, or seems to be, DIB (Dead in Bed) may be the ultimate kick in sex, but the vast majority of males want their females live and lively in the sack. And far too many women think it's enough to lie back, spread their legs, and let their partners do all the acting, reacting, and emoting. Not so. It takes two to tango, and it's up to the woman to do her equal share of moving and maneuvering.

Quite often a man can test his bed partner by taking her to a dance beforehand. If she's a good dancer, he can almost be assured of a good-moving lady in his bed. Once in bed, she ought to have the rhythmic movement of a tigress. She should be inventive and suggest different positions. For example: "Darling, how would it be if I turned with my ass against you and took you inside me from behind?" On the other hand, she should not wriggle all around the place like a fly in a bottle, or try to stage-manage the performance: "Now we'll do it standing up.... Now we'll do it on a rocking chair." This could be almost as big a turn-off as no movement at all. Indicate what you would like by moving your body subtly into various positions, and at the same time try to anticipate what you think he might like. If you want to be a sexually liberated woman, the first thing you should do is join the "woman's movement."

9. BEWITCHED, BEWILDERED, AND BEDDAZZLED. Sex symbols Paul Newman and Elizabeth Taylor were having marital problems in the scorching Tennessee Williams story *Cat on a Hot Tin Roof*, and were warned by her wise old mother-in-law, "When a marriage goes on the rocks, the rocks are right here in this bed." Of course, Big Mama's thought-provoking pearl of wisdom was meant figuratively. But let's take it literally. Maybe not many romances have been washed up because of bad bedding, but maybe it has happened more often than one might think. At any rate, we should not address ourselves to the subject of pleasuring the penis without giving consideration to the playpen in which the penis reigns supreme.

It stands to reason that, since we spend approximately one-third of our day-to-day life and almost all of our conventional sex life in bed, it should be a pleasant place to be. A woman's bed makes a big statement about her sexuality. If it's generous in size, well-arranged with lots of inviting pillows and feminine furbelows, it bespeaks a sexually oriented female. If it's messy, with unpressed or unlaundered sheets, it's a turn-off. From a man's point of view, generally speaking (there *are* exceptions), one of the most unappetizing of all domestic sights is an unmade bed.

A too-narrow bed discourages languid and loving fore- or afterplay, and a squeaky one is a distraction. Textures and colors of bedclothes count a lot, and while much depends on the taste of the individuals, I've noticed that the two most popular choices are the crisp white sheets that gave him so much security in his childhood—and were probably the background for his first memorable orgasms—and the complete reverse, black satin. While black satin isn't so restful for sleeping (for one thing, the pillows go spinning all over the place), it is very conducive to lovemaking. Often, too, I get my lover to lie face-down and slip and slide his body against my slinky black satin sheets until his penis is ready for more strenuous action.

You can add to the erotic atmosphere by sprinkling perfume between the sheets at thigh- or knee-level. Perfume on the pillow can be overpowering, but beneath the sheets, when he goes down on you, it can be overwhelming.

Paradoxical as it may sound, even the most romantic woman has a practical streak to her sexuality—based on the fact that it's better to be organized than unprepared. Alongside her bed she should keep certain fundamentals that eliminate the need to dash off to the bathroom and interrupt a mood of loving closeness. I call this survival package the "Clit Kit," and it contains: Kleenex (handy for wiping; even though they tend to stick and disintegrate, they are easier to keep around than small towels); lubricants for anal adventures and body anointing; body lotion, Vaseline or a tube of Nivea cream; her contraceptives, if she has to use them, and, ideally, a rubber for him in case it may be needed for emergency or for sexual variety; and her vibrator, also for emergencies and variety.

There is one other item that a girlfriend of mine

would not be without alongside her bed, and that is a sturdy string of beads. She does one of the oldest Oriental sex tricks with these. She greases her lover's anus with cream and inserts the beads slowly, as deeply as she can. While he is screwing her she pulls them out, one by one, controlling the pace of his lovemaking. Then, when she wants him to come, she abruptly jerks the rest of the string, giving him a thundering orgasm and one of the greatest sex thrills you can give your man.

You might call that pleasuring the penis through the rear door, but when it's done well, the penis will be delirious with pleasure. A little practice is all that's needed to attain proficiency. And even when it's done ineptly, it isn't bad at all!

10. NOTHING COULD BE FINER THAN TO BE IN YOUR VAGINA—IN THE MORNING. The "Morning Glory," so-called, has a sensuality all its own. It is usually the lovemaking that one partner initiates before the other is really awake. But since we're talking about pleasuring the penis, and since I've always maintained that the penis has a mind of its own, independent of the man attached to it, I have an even better suggestion.

While her partner is still fast asleep, the woman can carefully remove the covers and unbutton the fly of his pajamas, assuming he is so gauche as to be wearing the bottom half of his pajamas. Then she can gently start sucking his cock. He may only half-awaken, but his cock will be wide awake. From that point on it can be a prebreakfast blowjob or a good old-fashioned fuck—or both.

As a matter of fact, being sucked off while he's asleep is just about every man's fantasy. This can be carried one step further by inventing a dream. Tell him, "I dreamed you and I were in a restaurant and there was another couple at the table and the woman accidentally dropped her fork. As she bent down to pick it up, she noticed your fly was open, and she got so excited she crawled under the table and sucked you off. Everybody in the restaurant was watching, because the tablecloth was very short, and they could see what she was doing to you." Even if he suspects this is a figment of your invention, the idea will turn him on. It will do things for his penis' imagination—and you can do the rest for the penis itself.

ONE FOR GOOD MEASURE: INSIDE STUFF. Every sexually active woman—with the exception of post-hysterectomy and post-menopausal women—experiences times when having straight sex presents a problem. This brings up the very vital question of how to pleasure the penis at a time when the ordinary unsophisticated woman would simply shrug her shoulders and say, "Sorry; not tonight, Joseph."

The obvious no-entry occasions are, of course, every month when, as teen-age boys used to put it, "She's got the red flag flying." It could also occur postoperatively after a D and C (dilation and curettage), or after an abortion, when medical instructions warn her, "Don't put anything inside your vagina for two weeks."

If the relationship is a brand-new one, it becomes awkward and sometimes even a turn-off if she has to explain the clinical details of her indisposition. If it's a long-existing love partnership, it can become a monthly and tedious exercise to explain, "Not today, dear." (For professional females it can be an economic disaster.) There has to be an alternative. There is. Here's how to "overcome."

1. Have anal sex, provided she can enjoy it, using creams or Vaseline to lubricate the opening. A lot of women call this "the agony and the ecstasy." If it's the first time for her, he has to take it slowly and gently to get beyond the taut anal sphincter muscle without causing her too much pain.

2. If anal sex is out, she lies on her stomach and he smooths pools of fragrant body lotion on and between her buttocks. Then he fucks the deep lubricated valley between her cheeks.

3. She lies on her back, rubs lots of body lotion around her breasts, holds them together so they form a moist cleft, and he fucks her breasts. When he comes, she has a warm sperm bath around her chest and chin.

4. When the "indisposition" is menstrual, she performs oral sex on him, and assuming he is an unselfish lover who can enjoy complete satisfaction only if she is also sexually cared for, he performs it on her—after she douches, inserts her diaphragm, and douches again. He can then eat her without even knowing she has her period.

5. What if he doesn't want to accept any substitutes for straight intercourse? Provided her problem is menstrual and not medical, she can have internal sex by (a) inserting a small tampon into her vagina; or (b) taking a surgical sponge, wetting it, wringing the water out, and inserting it high up against the uterus,

then making love and removing it immediately after; or (c) taking a large wad of cotton, coating it generously with Vaseline, and inserting it the same way as the sponge. The sponge is easily retrievable, but the cotton may not be; however, with a little time, it works its way down and out of the vagina.

When all is said and done, no deserving penis need go unpleasured at any time or under any circumstances. And as far as I'm concerned, there are no undeserving penises.

CHAPTER TEN

A Pleasure Chest of Sex Toys, OR, Try These for Openers

I have always said that if I had a cock I would want it to be the biggest one possible and I'd go around with a hard-on all the time and screw every attractive girl in sight. (This shows how inconsistent we all are about sex; I've said dozens of times that size doesn't make that much difference, and yet, I know that if I had a cock I'd *still* want it to be a big one.) However, the urge to play the role of the opposite sex is not a fantasy of only women. There's also such a thing as "cunt envy," and I've encountered it many times. Well, in these enterprising days, where there's an urge there's always an entrepreneur or two to satisfy it, at a price. The proprietor of your local sex-toy shop will sell you an artificial penis if you lack one, a penis enlarger if you have a small one, a penis enhancer if you want to get fancy, an artificial vagina, and in fact virtually anything your wildest fantasy can conjure up, including an artificial man or woman.

Being a bit on the chintzy side, I must admit I'm more likely to borrow than to buy any artificial devices I might want to employ. For example, I once had a freaky affair with a male movie star who had this fantasy that he was my whore and wanted me to fuck him, instead of vice versa. First of all, I titillated him by putting my tongue in his anus, then I progressed to inserting my lubricated fingers, and afterward to the Japanese trick of inserting a string of beads, as described in another chapter, because I knew he was quite sensitive in that area. Then I borrowed a strap-on dildo from a lesbian friend and fucked him up his ass with it while I masturbated his penis at the same time. He told me this was one of the most exciting episodes he had ever had in his life, and he was hardly a young innocent.

That particular dildo was made of rather firm rubber and had a nodule that sort of rubbed against my clitoris and stimulated me at the same time, not that I reached an orgasm, because I don't really get off with artificial cocks. However, one woman's cold comfort may be another woman's best friend. Needless to say, the variety in dildo models is limitless.

I once saw a stag show in Denmark in which the girl had a double-ended rubber dildo that was the size of a healthy penis and had a big head on each end. Are you ready? She fucked herself in the ass with one end and stuffed the other up her cunt, and even though she was in front of an audience, she really seemed to enjoy herself. Another scene I saw was between two lesbians who sat facing each other, legs around waists, shoemaker style. These girls had a long, long double-headed dildo which they slid in and out, up and down, without even touching it with their hands, so that the audience could see everything. Either they used a bucketful of lubricant or they were very turned on, because they sure generated a lot of juice.

Modern sex performers, exhibitionists, freaks, and imaginative lovers were certainly not the first to discover penis substitutes and enhancers. Fops of the fifteenth and sixteenth centuries, for example, wore what was called a "codpiece" that emphasized the genitals behind them. This was often an embroidered patch attached outside the man's trousers, and its size bore little relationship to the actual appendage it concealed.

The Eskimos, too, had it all worked out. While everybody thought they only rubbed noses, I found out that the women rubbed long penises made out of whalebone against their clitorises, which their considerate husbands carved and left behind as wife pacifiers while they went out hunting.

There's another toy that some emancipated husbands give their wives to play with while they're away on trips, so the wives won't feel the need to cheat. These are called ben-wah balls, and it won't surprise anybody that they were invented by the inventive Japanese, who seem to have thought of every kind of cunt and cock substitute or stimulator under the rising sun. There are two balls, usually made of metal or a specially weighted plastic, about the size of smallish Ping-Pong balls, with a string attached for easy retrieval. They have to be inserted, with lubricant, inside the vagina and are supposed to be one of the greatest friction stimulators imaginable. I've heard that a woman can have repeated and prolonged clitoral orgasms if she walks around with ben-wah balls inside her. However, I tried them once when a girlfriend of mine, who owns a sex shop in Toronto, gave me a pair because she considers me a good ad for her shop. I didn't like them much; in fact, they just felt uncomfortable to me. But when my girlfriend used them in a half-hour plane ride, she found that even though she was restricted to wriggling around in her seat she had a really good time. These things work better when the woman is swinging back and forth in a hammock or when she is swimming. And if you ever see a woman with a big smile on her face as she rocks back and forth in a rocking chair, it may just be because her ben-wah balls are working well.

Penis and pussy substitutes come in all different shapes and sizes, from dildoes to vibrators and artificial mouths and vaginas. There are so many, in fact, that it would take a whole yellow-page directory to list them. Nevertheless, I've compiled a consumer report to give guidance to those who want to add an extra dimension to their sex lives but aren't sure what to look for. But first of all, a lot of shoppers must overcome their bashfulness. I'm always hearing, "I would love to buy one of those French ticklers, but I'm too shy to ask for it." Don't be; that's what these sex shops—and now there are even sex supermarkets—are there for. They don't care if you buy six rubber penises, any more than Neiman-Marcus would care if you bought three green elephants. When I lived in New York I used to go to Forty-second Street, where they have all the hot sex shops; even though they deal in porn material, the owner would quite often have a special private collection of even pornier items under the counter. I would simply say I wanted some whips, chains, and manacles. Not that it was any of their business, but usually I explained, "I'm a hooker, and this is my specialty."

For women, naturally, the sex items are designed to stimulate the vagina or the clitoris. There are countless kinds of vibrators that can be used for solitary enjoyment, or together with one's lover, male or female, as a turn-on. One vibrator, which is a legitimate electrical appliance and is sold as such, attaches to the back of the hand rather than to the front. The woman uses her own palm to stroke her lover's body, giving him exciting vibrations all over.

Most vibrators, though, are shaped like penises. However, I recently came across some rectal stimulators, as well as a collection of vibrator sleeves shaped like fingers, cucumbers, spirals, and dogs' penises. There's one rubber sleeve that has horizontal rows of soft rubber spikes a couple of inches apart. The combination vibrator-dildo I like to use is about the size of two fingers held together; it has a small battery inside and is great to apply against the clitoris when your man is on top and fucking you while your legs are around his shoulders. That way you get double stimulation.

There are many remarkable penis simulations, complete with "veins" and a shaft of movable skinlike material. These range in size from a modest six inches to an outrageous twelve inches, which the manufacturer calls "Mr. Destroyer." There's also another one that has pliable wire inside so that madam can bend it to her favorite shape. This monster measures fifteen inches, and they call it "the wire mule—just for kicks." Then there's a series of artificial cocks that are not battery-operated but have a twisting handle instead. These rotate with a spiral motion, and a woman can literally screw herself by simply turning the handle. They are available in different shapes and sizes.

For women who want to screw each other, there are dozens of dildoes available, but most of these need to be strapped on firmly. It might be a good idea to purchase a sort of universal harness, which has a strap that goes around the back and under the crotch; this device accommodates most shapes and sizes. Another fascinating item I've come across is made exclusively for oral activity. This is a man's face, complete with facial hairs, eyebrows, and a nice thick moustache, all built out of lifelike rubber. The face has a long tongue protruding from the mouth, and this contains miniature batteries. By pressing the face to her crotch, a woman gets a terrific tongue job from a mouth that never tires. There are also women's faces with long pink battery-operated tongues for women with lesbian preferences who don't quite have the courage to go out and try a real girl.

For the man, there are women's faces with lush lips and battery-stimulated mouths into which he can insert his cock. This way he can have a never-ending blowjob. This plastic pet can hold out as long as he can—and then some. They also sell men's mustachioed faces for male-oriented men. Then there are artificial vaginas that men can use when they are alone, and there's another type that the woman can strap onto herself at times when she's indisposed.

With these attachments, a couple can have full body contact without cock and cunt contact. It all sounds a bit too mechanized to me, but there are plenty of people who dig this sort of thing. They are available with or without hair. There's also a life-sized doll made of stuffed plastic material; it has a hairy cunt that juices itself, on pressure, with a special lubrication. It never has a headache and it never talks back. These are fairly costly, and the price varies with the model—black, white, or Oriental; naked or wearing lingerie.

Rubber rings; decorated condoms, or French ticklers; cock caps, or penis extenders, are next on the list—for him to give extra excitement to her. The rubber rings are mainly designed to go around the middle of the shaft of the penis and create tickling sensations inside the vagina by way of protruding rubbery spikes, little frondlike projections, or small rubber studs. There's another kind that is worn around the base of the penis that stimulates the entire vulva, labia, and clitoris with a continuous gentle friction while he makes love to her. With all these rings and constricting devices, the man must make sure they are not too tight; otherwise he might cause vein congestion and injure himself.

There's a whole set of cock caps that fit over the head of the penis; these are made of soft rubber, and there's no limit to the bizarre decorations available. While you're at it, add these to your condom shopping list: a Mexican hat, a devil's face, a rooster, a bursting sunflower, a super nipple, a green Christmas tree, a cactus, a mushroom, an octopus, a rosebud, and a so-called tongue fish. There are also "disappearing" condoms that contain a spermicide; the whole condom dissolves during intercourse but remains effective as a contraceptive because of the spermicidal effect.

The Orientals have been in the vanguard in the never-ending quest for penis elongators, and once more the Japanese are far out in front. They have designed a vacuum-type tube, which, when applied to the penis, sucks it forward and is supposed to endow it with added length. However, that silly millimeter longer could make its owner's life a few years shorter, because it has a dangerous effect on the blood circulation in the penis. With great ingenuity, the Japanese have also devised lifelike rubber cylinders that slip over the penis, giving it more length and width, that absolutely defy detection. There are also various artificial penises and penis attachments that have hollow scrotums that contain warm liquid and shoot it out through a pipe in the shaft.

In the art of penismanship there are all kinds of substitutes, compensations, and added attractions. Some men know how to use them to their own, and the woman's, best advantage, and some almost kill themselves trying. I'm talking about drugs and alcohol and their use and abuse as mind-blowers and leg openers. The search for a reliable aphrodisiac is as old as the pursuit of the fountain of youth, and just as frustrating.

The Chinese have applied a great deal of characteristic patience and ingenuity to discovering potency-increasing substances, and to this day they believe it exists in such stratagems as leaving a fresh olive in the vagina of a virgin overnight and in such ingredients as powdered rhinoceros horn and various foodstuffs, from snake soup to walnuts. However, a girlfriend of mine did a little bit of snooping around at the famous sex show in Macao, which is near Hong Kong. She discovered that the only special nourishment used by the sex exhibitionist who had been performing before a live audience, screwing as often as six times a day for the last ten years, was cans and cans of Horlicks malted milk!

Actually, there is no true aphrodisiac; but there are mood-changers and disinhibitors that act on the nerve centers that control sexual response and performance. The most common of all, of course, is booze. This acts more or less as a disinhibitor at first, alleviating shyness and helping the man or woman overcome anxieties in a new situation. However, there are three things to remember about alcohol: the safe intake is in direct ratio to the body weight of the drinker; tolerance decreases with age—if a man has been handling a three-martini lunch all his life and becomes perplexed when, all of a sudden, he can't cope with it anymore, age is probably the reason; and alcohol is quite addictive—the more you drink, the more you want. And one more thing is that if it's overdone it's a real bore for the partner. I saw this quite a lot in my house in New York, especially among the Irish and Scots, who would often come in drunk and were difficult customers. Not only were they very demanding and noisy, but they would practically screw you to pieces because they could not come. They could keep a hard-on for hours and would blame the girls, when it was really the alcohol they should have blamed for their delayed or nonexistent ejaculation. So, while a glass or two of alcohol may be a relaxant, the best you can say about too much is that it cures premature ejaculation—and how!

Another popular sex heightener is amyl nitrite, or the so-called "popper," which dilates the blood vessels and therefore increases the blood flow to the heart. A popper is used at the moment of male orgasm; usually the woman snaps open the little glass ampule under the man's nose, and he has a terrifically intensified orgasm. However, he can also get a terrifically throbbing headache. And that's not its only drawback. You can bring on severe dizziness if you stand while taking this drug, because it can cause a sudden drop in blood pressure and a racing heart. And anyone with glaucoma should steer clear of this drug, because it can result in a dangerous increase in pressure within the eye. I've also heard it on good authority that liquor and amyl nitrite don't mix; the combination can bring on "nitrite syncope," a severe shocklike state. I don't think amyl nitrite and sado-masochists are a good mixture, either. Once I used it on a freak in a sado-masochist scene in New York, and the customer went off his head. He beat me black and blue, and I ended up in a hospital. That particular experience may have been his own freak-out rather than the amyl nitrite, but the drug could have contributed to it, too.

Something called the "love drug" can have a similar intensifying effect on male orgasm. However, there are any number of drugs referred to by this name, some quite hazardous, so you should be wary of anything offered as a "love drug." Among the various love drugs are cocaine, strychnine—which is often used as a rat poison and can easily kill a human—and PCP, a horse tranquilizer. PCP has a tendency to give a man a hard-on for a long time. In some cases he won't be able to reach orgasm, but it gives him a very lovely feeling if he does come with it. And even when he doesn't, he feels very groovy. But you take it at your own risk, unless you're a horse.

Hard drugs have liabilities that far outweigh the pleasure of using them for sexual enhancement. I've tried cocaine, which slows everything down and seems to increase the sexual sensations and performance. Men have told me it is very exciting but that it also makes them sort of numb, delaying ejaculation considerably. Eventually, a psychological addiction and craving for this very expensive drug takes over (though it's not physically addictive), and the user becomes more preoccupied with getting his dose of coke than with giving his lover a length of cock, which is certainly self-defeating. Heroin is even worse, because it *is* physically addictive, and I wouldn't touch it with a three-foot dildo.

Barbiturates have given me funny experiences. One I remember especially well occurred with my former boyfriend Larry while we were doing the town in Paris. We were both feeling as horny as beans and looking for that extra little bit of excitement to go with it. First we went to a fine French restaurant and then on to a swank discothèque, where somebody gave us a couple of barbiturates with the warning, "Have a good time, but whatever you do, don't close your eyes or the fun will be over." We went running back to our hotel ready for the best fuck of our lives. While Larry was in the bathroom brushing his teeth, I lay down for a second. The next thing I remember was waking up next morning, fully dressed from the night before, with Larry asleep beside me. Barbiturates are classified as hypnotics; they depress the central nervous system, have no specific sex elevators, are temporary disinhibitors, and are dangerously addictive, to the extent that the user eventually does not even want to have sex.

I don't recommend any kind of drugs to anyone, but I must be honest and admit that, personally, I prefer to get stoned on mescaline. Mescaline, which comes in many forms—tablets, powders, mushroom-like mescal buttons, and even liquid—causes hallucinations and an alteration in perception, though, like LSD, the exact effect can't be predicted. In fact, there's nothing predictable about a mescaline trip. It can create a feeling of emotional, physical, and sexual intimacy—and when it does, it's great—but there's no guarantee that it will have this effect. You can have a fantastic trip, but occasionally it can be an extremely heavy and even a traumatic experience, especially with synthetic mescaline, because much of what is sold as synthetic mescaline is really LSD, speed, or almost anything else. Genuine synthetic mescaline, on the other hand, produces an experience quite like the real stuff, minus the nausea and severe retching some people experience with natural mescaline, which tastes vile.

Experiences vary, but for me, if I have a nice trip on mescaline, it's generally a truth trip and it becomes very hard to lie or deceive anyone. For instance, I remember once I was making love with my boyfriend, whom I had cheated on a few times over the past couple of weeks. I hadn't told him, because I didn't want to hurt his feelings. However, when I was stoned, I told him, "I fucked so-and-so and so-and-so." Just like that. Luckily, he was as stoned as I was and just shrugged it off with a giggle. Ordinarily, that confession would have infuriated him.

I've also found that my senses get keener on a mescaline trip, and everything is enlarged and exaggerated. When I was sucking my lover's cock it seemed three times as big, and so did my tits. I watched while he was kissing them, and I looked like Sophia Loren. But on another trip, or for someone else, everything could well have been exaggerated to the opposite extreme.

THC, which is the product that results from synthesizing the active ingredient (TetraHydroCannabinol) found in both hash and grass, has much the same effect as marihuana or hashish, though it is often stronger. The length of a THC trip, as with all drugs sold on the street, depends on the dosage, and, again, you can't count on having specific reactions. Some of the THC (and mescaline) I've had must have been part amphetamine, because everything seemed speeded up and the orgasm became secondary to the experience of sex.

LSD is another hallucinogen that changes perception and loosens inhibitions. Couples screwing on this have told me that the experience was so dazzling, with colored lights and beautiful sounds, that it was like making love in your own private cinema with the film *2001: A Space Odyssey* going full blast. However, LSD is also a different trip for different people. Many have reported they didn't like the way it continued to mess up their perceptions after they came down. It is said to work on the central systems of the brain, and that isn't something I'd want to tamper with, though recent evidence suggests that so-called "flashbacks" rarely occur and were greatly exaggerated in the drug literature of the late 1960's.

Marihuana is believed to be a mild sex stimulant and emotional disinhibitor, and a trip on grass is like a trip to Puerto Rico. Everybody's been there! I enjoy it now and again, although I'm not much of a smoker. Most pot smokers, though, say that it makes them feel more sensuous, erotic, and uninhibited, and makes them longer-performing and slower-ejaculating. It seems to prolong the orgasmic feeling and intensify the pulsations, though this is primarily a matter of altered perception. Whether marihuana actually has that effect or not hardly seems important when you consider the pleasure you get from whatever really happens on its own merits.

Some researchers, however, have lately come up with the conclusion that what you get at the party you may pay for afterward. They did a survey on a hundred or so college kids who were marihuana smokers and found a loss of masculinity in which the blood level of the male hormone, testosterone, was forty-four percent lower than in nonsmokers. Thirty-five percent of the tea-heads had reduced sperm counts, which were restored to normal two weeks after they stopped smoking grass. They also concluded that smoking may literally stunt one's growth, because the preadolescent who uses pot may deprive himself of the hormones needed to make him into an adult male. Although these results are not widely accepted and have not yet been duplicated in further experiments, it's an indication that marihuana *may* be harmful. There's also some fear it could have adverse effects on a male fetus if the mother smokes pot during the critical weeks of gestation.

One of my most unforgettable trips of all time was on amphetamines, otherwise known as speed or diet pills. This drug makes you feel light, forget your problems, and talk compulsively. There's nothing worse than staying home alone when you take speed, because you need to talk, talk, and talk, and that was where my troubles began. This was the now-famous shoplifting incident, when I was arrested and charged with stealing from a Vancouver department store. What the press and the public didn't know was that I was two feet off the ground on a big speed trip. I had taken two pills, had to get out of my hotel room for a while, and decided to get my rocks off by shoplifting. I suppose this is true kleptomania, because my desire to steal was very neurotic and beyond my emotional control. The judge did not quite see it that way, and as most people know, I was charged and convicted.

The freaky thing about the episode was that I was aware I was being tailed by a woman detective and a male detective, who were watching all my movements. I had already taken a nightdress and deliberately picked up another couple of items, knowing all along that if I at any time decided to drop this merchandise in a fitting room or casually leave it somewhere in the store, there was nothing they could do about it. I was aware that I was not acting illegally until I actually crossed the line separating the store property from the street. Nevertheless, I was off on a mad chase, zigzagging giddily back and forth between the counters and onto the escalators, the way kids sometimes do. I wanted to escape, and at the same time, I wanted to get caught. I could see the front entrance of the store before me and the daylight streaming through, so I quickened my pace. So did the two detectives. The second I stepped across that forbidden border I felt their hands clamp down on my shoulders. And, at that instant, I was riveted to the ground, squeezing my legs together tightly, and my panties were soaked with my "come."

Possibly the most classic of all aphrodisiacs is the famous Spanish fly, which does genuinely help you get it up, in a roundabout way. Left to its own devices, the penis becomes erect when the blood vessels within it dilate. Spanish fly abets erection by irritating the bladder and the urethra, which in turn causes the erection mechanism to function, sometimes to the point of no return. Priapism, or continuing erection, is one result of Spanish fly. Another result is permanent penis and bladder damage, which is more or less an itch that you'll spend the rest of your life scratching, and never quite getting relief.

A substance that many regard as a true aphrodisiac is androgen testosterone, which seems to increase desire and drive in both men and women. Doctors have been using it with some success in the treatment of chronic impotence, although, by and large, the medical profession is skeptical about this effect of androgen testosterone. And, as with any sex stimulus you get from over or under the counter, out of a bottle, or in a packet of pills, there are certain drawbacks. Being a male hormone, this substance can create a susceptibility to prostate cancer in men; in women it's not that bad, but still not good. Many women suffer severe attacks of acne, and others grow hair where they least want it.

Penismanship, or making the most of what you've got, seems to be the only reliable leg-opener. Not that I don't enjoy a kick with a dildo or a joint of grass or what-have-you every now and again. However, I think a man who knows how to use his own joint to its best advantage will lead a fuller sex life in the long run. I've opened up the pleasure chest of sex toys for you in this chapter, but I still recommend doing what comes naturally—as set forth by your faithful sex correspondent in all of the other chapters.

CHAPTER ELEVEN

A Treasury of Orgasms, OR, How to Come in Nine Languages

It will probably never win a place in *Bartlett's Familiar Quotations*, but possibly the favorite phrase in the English language these days is, "Honey, I'm coming!"

Just why the male ejaculate came to be called "come" or how that particular notification of an important impending event evolved, nobody, including myself, seems to know. All I know is, everybody's doing it, and most of us are saying it. Maybe the explanation is very simple. It could be that some demon lover of the past whispered passionately, "Honey, I'm arriving!" and the girl laughed so hard she fell out of bed.

Of course, the English-speaking countries don't have a copyright on the expression. In my own country, Holland, we say *Ik kom klaar*, which means literally, "I'm coming now." In France it's *J'y arrive!* Italy, *Ora vengo!* or *Vengo, vengo!* or *Arrivo!* (I arrive). The Germans pant *Ich komme gleich!* (I'm coming right now). Portuguese, *Quero gozar!* (I'm going to come) or *Eston gozando!* (I am coming). Russians, *Ja budu gotovy!* Greeks, *Erchome!* Hungarians, *Jaj de joesik el sulta pinam!* And now, are you ready for the Japanese? By them, it's *Iku, iku!* or *Quoi, quoi, quoi!*

While I prefer a verbal comer, there are some men who just make interesting sounds, like moans and groans. My favorite lover of the moment sounds like a thunderstorm coming up just before he tells me he's coming. It sounds like "*Errrrrrrrr!*" (it's impossible to duplicate his sound), and it really turns me on. There are also some men who say absolutely nothing at all. They just pant a little harder.

Anyway, this chapter is all about orgasms. And if that isn't worth this entire chapter, if not a book, I don't know what is. One of the lovely things about sex in general and orgasms in particular is the fact that everybody is different, no matter how slight the difference. I've noticed that about the one reaction shared by all men is that they curl up their toes when they're coming. (Not easy to observe in the missionary position, but there are other positions and postures.) Apart from that, there's infinite variety in the way men feel, the way they express their emotions, the amount of "come" they ejaculate (the way it tastes, how it looks—does it squirt or trickle), and how long it takes them to reach climax.

There's a myth that the man who can fuck and maintain a hard-on for an hour is a great lover. The truth is, most women don't really care for marathon sex; it's a turn-off, because after twenty minutes of pumping in and out, she gets damn sore and exhausted. Ideal lovemaking, like anything else, shouldn't last too long or end too soon. I shouldn't really put a time limit on it, because there are so many exceptions, but if you pinned me down, I'd say it shouldn't last much longer than fifteen minutes or end in less than five minutes.

However, there are many men who can't last even five minutes. (It's a longer interval than it sounds—when you're fucking.) With them it's National Stud Day if they manage to make it to the inside of the woman's vagina. There was, for example, the man I met after I got out of the prostitution business: the girls called him "The Hookers' Delight" because he'd pay his money and come in less than a minute. He was the fastest, easiest lay they ever had. When I was introduced to him I said, "Look, honey, I can't believe you get any fun from coming in a minute like that, nor can you be giving your partner much fun. I'm not a hooker anymore, and I'd like to give you some genuine pleasure." We lay on the bed, and I stroked and caressed him and applied some oral action, and when he was overcome with excitement, I diverted his attention with something suitably neutral. "What did you do over the weekend?" I asked him. He said he went horseback riding, and we talked about that for a while—not long, a minute or so—then I started turning him on again. After about ten minutes of attract-distract foreplay, I let him insert his penis into my vagina. Naturally, this got him very excited, so I brought up the topic of the stock market, which was very depressed at the time; I also applied squeeze pressure in my vagina, and he was able to hold back awhile longer. Then I let him have another couple of good strong strokes, and then asked him about the play he had seen the night before. This may not have been the most scientific method of dealing with premature ejaculation, but at least I made "The

Hookers' Delight" last six minutes inside me, which was six times longer than he'd ever lasted in his whole life!

Premature ejaculation is about the most common of all male sex dysfunctions, and sex clinics are sprouting up all over the place to treat it. Some therapists say it is caused by anxiety about pleasing the partner, and in the case of a wife who does not understand her husband's deep worry over the problem, it just gets worse. For example, the man may appear distant or a little indifferent when he makes love, but the whole point is that he's doing what he *should* be doing—deliberately *avoiding* concentrating on her beautiful, voluptuous body. She might feel bewildered, rejected, and angry, and unless he is candid with her, they might develop a permanent pattern of frustration. It was said by Freud that some men come prematurely because they harbor a deep-seated, unconscious hostility toward all women and this is their way of depriving women of pleasure. If a man feels, consciously or unconsciously, that sex is somewhat dirty, then premature ejaculation is also a device for "soiling" her with his "come."

The man's premature tendencies may have been aggravated by his first experiences with a hooker who humiliated him with "Hurry it up, kid!" or "Boy, next time I won't bother to open my legs!" Or maybe it was his teen-age girlfriend on the back seat of the car, forcing him to rush because she was afraid somebody would catch them at it.

On rare occasions, premature ejaculation, or PE, as I'll call it from now on, is caused by a physical disorder. My doctor friends tell me this could be a break in the nerve-system circuit that controls the penis sensations; or, if it is a sudden problem, it may be prostatitis, in which case most men would see blood in their ejaculate or experience some pain associated with coming. PE is much more likely to be mental than physical. Whatever the cause—hostility, performance anxiety, anticipation of failure, or whatever—literally millions of men worry themselves sick and almost destroy their sex lives over this condition.

At what point does PE stop being PE and become merely the trait of a rather quick ejaculator? Even the clinical experts seem unable to answer this question precisely. One doctor says it's PE if thirty seconds or less elapse between vaginal insertion and ejaculation; another says two minutes is the telltale minimum, while a third says if a man ejaculates before ten thrusts, he's a preemie. I'm more charitable. I would say that a premature ejaculator is the man who comes before he even touches the female body, or as a result of moderate foreplay, or at the moment his penis enters her vagina. Maybe he comes on the first or the fourth stroke, which is early, but I think anything after six or seven strokes is not really a sign of PE but of a quick ejaculator.

All kinds of remedies have been tried, from applying anesthetic ointment or using thick condoms to diminish the penis sensations, to cold showers, or masturbation before intercourse. One method I used in my brothel was to encourage the man to concentrate on a depressing image while screwing. For instance, I would say, "Think of your aunt's funeral." But the only method so far that has had a consistently high permanent cure rate is the Semans method.

This is not named for the sperm, or semen, but for Dr. James Semans, the urologist who developed it. You might call it the "green-light–red-light" technique, because the man is turned on, then off, and then on again. The couple is told to set up a situation where they are at home in bed, naked, and the wife is asked to stimulate the penis manually or orally until he feels the sensation of an approaching orgasm. Then he lets her know, and she stops immediately. He now has to turn away from her and concentrate his attention solely on the physical sensations in his penis. He cannot, under any circumstances, think about the woman, since much of his ejaculation anxiety is created by what he thinks she is thinking. He is also not allowed to permit any thoughts of any kind to distract him from his exclusive focus on his penis. Strangely enough, this kind of concentration is actually anorgasmic, that is, tending to slow up the orgasm. After he gives his partner the red light and has concentrated on his sensations, he notices that the sensation of impending orgasm disappears in a few seconds. But before he loses his hard-on he gives her the green light and the turn-on–turn-off process is repeated again and again, until the fourth time, when he is permitted to ejaculate. He is also warned that at no point should he try to consciously control the orgasm, except for giving his wife the signal to stop or start him.

After the couple has completed this exercise on two occasions, the man is told to place a guiding hand over his wife's hand and experiment with the feelings created by alternating the speed and pressure on the shaft. When he has learned to recognize, without anxiety, the intense sensation that develops immediately before orgasm, and to be able to stop his wife in time, they do the whole thing with Vaseline on her hand instead of a dry run; this simulates the inside of a vagina to some extent. If all goes as desired, they then progress to normal intercourse, still using the Semans method until the man has overcome his PE.

There's another technique called karezza, developed by the Oneida community (a famous nineteenth-century experimental commune) to control pregnancy. In this system, the man and woman make love but he is permitted only sufficient strokes to keep his erection intact, and the rest—the muscular manipulation—is done by the woman. Of course, she must develop excellent vaginal skills so that she can, with the contractions of her vagina, "milk" and stroke while the male moves hardly at all. This can go on for quite a while, and when well executed, might come under the heading of "unendurable pleasure indefinitely prolonged." The man avoids ejaculation during intercourse, but while the effect is the same as coitus interruptus, the technique spares him the disagreeable chore of sudden withdrawal. The male partner learns to derive his pleasure from prolonged intimate contact with the woman rather than from an explosive orgasm. He may have an orgasm after withdrawal, but it will be a gentle one, almost a postscript to the leisurely act of lovemaking.

Going to the opposite extreme of PE, there are men who have gotten control down to too much of a fine art. Frankly, a man can be a real drag if he takes forever to come. One type I don't much care for is the one who says, "Don't worry about me, honey; I don't come. I can control it for hour after hour." You might as well get yourself a fucking machine as make love with him. Then again, there are plenty of men who suffer from what is called retarded ejaculation, or ejaculatory incompetence. This means he may have an occasional episode when, no matter how he does it, what he thinks of, or how long he goes at it, he cannot come. There are also men who have never had an orgasm, ever, in their life!

At one time, sex therapists thought retarded ejaculation was a relatively rare problem, but these days they say there's an incredible number of patients seeking help for just this problem. The condition can be caused by physical problems, such as extreme fatigue, or the scar tissue that forms on the urethra as a result of a dose of gonorrhea. In these situations, some men actually experience what is called "dry orgasm," when they enjoy the intense orgasmic sensation but minus the sperm.

Retarded ejaculation may occur when a man is with some women and not with others. The man's ejaculatory mechanism can be blocked, for example, with a woman who makes him feel anxious, guilty, or hostile. On the other hand, she may just have a rather slack vagina, possibly because she has had a bunch of kids in quick succession without taking good care of herself. Her pussy just won't provide sufficient friction; his penis is like a fish swimming in a bowl of water.

If a woman wants to speed things up, a good trigger-puller for the male orgasm is for the woman to insert her lubricated finger into his anus and gently stroke the prostate gland. Another way is for her to flatter his ego and fake it a little if he's taking too long. With most normal men, his pleasure has a lot to do with giving her pleasure, so if she moans and groans he'll start to feel good as long as he doesn't realize it's a white lie.

There are some women who are such bad actresses and carry on so much, scratching the backs of their partners and all, that the man knows it's obviously a fake. After all, if a man knows from his past experiences with other women that he's not really the last of the red hot lovers, he will more than suspect that this chili-pepper pussy lying under him apparently coming all over the place is something of a phony.

A man who's been around can tell from facial expressions whether his partner is enjoying it or not. If she's making all the right sounds but is just staring at the ceiling, she's probably on a big fib-trip. If she closes her eyes, it's harder to tell. She may be thinking of a chocolate-mint ice-cream cone, for all you know.

My lover usually knows when I'm faking it, if, for instance, he's made love to me for a long time and I've already come once or twice. Then I just say, "Oh, that was nice." I really don't fake the orgasms; I just don't let him know that I'd like to call it quits. I want to be honest, but I just don't want to tell him I've gotten a bit sore and he's hurting me; I want him to come too. He can tell afterward, from my lukewarm response, that the grand finale wasn't so grand for me.

When a woman is really turned on, just before she

reaches orgasm her nipples will generally stand up stiffer than ever. She might even develop goose bumps all over her body, especially on the breasts and upper legs. And if the man is performing oral sex, he can feel her coming if he knows the score; he can actually feel the clitoris grow in his mouth. She'll become more lubricated as well, except for the woman who is on the pill, in which case she normally doesn't lubricate as much. With my man, sometimes his shaft is completely covered with my whitish secretion. His sperm goes in much deeper and leaks out later when I get up. But when a man's shaft is wet all the way to the base, he can practically be guaranteed a woman has come. Of course, she doesn't come in a big squashy jetstream like a man, though some women do have extremely heavy secretions.

To reverse it, how does a woman recognize if a man is really coming or, as with some retarded ejaculators, faking it? It's pretty difficult for a man to pretend orgasm, for the simple reason that, even if the woman doesn't feel the actual jet, when she gets up after making love she'll feel his sperm drip out of her vagina. A man may say he has just masturbated a few hours earlier and didn't have any semen left. Wrong. The amount is almost exactly the same; it may just be weaker in sperm count. If a woman is very moist herself, a man can take advantage of that and pretend he's had an orgasm; she may be confused between her own fluid and his, especially if she stays in bed afterward and goes right to sleep.

Another form of faking is quite common with male studs or male prostitutes. They are required to perform frequent sexual acts, generally by giving it to their clients from the rear end. They may do this as often as five or six times a day, and it would be physically impossible to reach full orgasm every time. In this situation the stud can just fake it, and once the client reaches his orgasm, the stud can just pull out with a semi-hard-on or a full hard-on and be ready for the next customer in a short while.

There's a famous story that says the world's three biggest lies are: "The check's in the mail," "Of course I love you," and "I promise I won't come in your mouth." How does she know if he's telling the truth? When the man is on the brink of shooting his sperm while she's giving him head, she can feel his penis grow in her mouth to such a degree that the head swells up and the balls become tighter and almost seem to disappear into the body. Then the whole penis gets steel-rigid—and the toes curl up! If he makes love to her inside her body, it will be more difficult to guess, but you get a pretty good idea from his harder breathing and convulsive gripping with his hands. And, of course, there are always those famous words: "Honey, I'm coming!"

How many times can a man come in a given period of time? This depends on the health and age of the individual and on how long he takes to replenish, because certain body-manufacturing processes slow down as a person gets older. Kinsey had one young man in his report who claimed he could have four rapid-fire erections to orgasm, spaced only ten minutes apart. But most normally functioning men should not feel intimidated by that statistic. I would say that men between their early twenties and mid-forties should be able to produce enough sperm to ejaculate once an hour over a three-hour period. In my opinion, a man's best time for repeater-style lovemaking is the matinee, between two and five in the afternoon after a *light* lunch.

If you think we've discussed everything about the orgasm that there is to consider, don't forget we haven't yet gotten to the subject of household hints. In other words, how do you get the male ejaculate out of fabrics? A dry-cleaner friend of mine told me people are always too embarrassed to identify the specific stains as "come," but as he says, he doesn't have to be Louis Pasteur to figure out the origin of a suspicious white splotch on a man's trouser front. This is strictly no problem for a professional. However, if you don't happen to be making love in a laundry, you should let it dry (sperm coagulates immediately on ejaculation, liquefies ten minutes later, then dries). Then you take a dry toothbrush and scrub it off. If it's your good velvet sofa—or, much worse, your best friend's wife's sofa—you can still try the toothbrush method. If that doesn't work, take a little water and soap and hope for the best.

Some people believe that semen is endowed with magical properties that provide nutrition and a cure for acne. Actually, semen does contain protein, citric acid, and certain sugars, along with several other constituents. I was told that the Chinese girls in Hong Kong, who remain young and beautiful well into their middle years, especially value their frequent internal injections, both oral and vaginal, of health-giving sperm.

As to whether it's actually good for the skin, I'll

leave that to the doctors. But if you want a diet that really works, remember that semen contains only one calorie per serving—and it's infinitely more fun than yoghurt.

CHAPTER TWELVE

Getting Your Money's Worth in a Brothel, OR, Joint Negotiations

Everybody used to say my house in New York was just like a home away from home, with one exception—the girls. While my customers loved to relax in the comfortable homelike surroundings, they demanded variety in bed partners. After all, that's why most of them were there in the first place. So it was with some surprise that I sought out the right girl for a customer whom I'll call Stammering Sam. This man was slim, bespectacled, shy, and quite a stutterer, and my madam's instinct told me he was most likely married to a wife of a similar type. Nevertheless, when he managed to stammer out his request for a "s-s-s-s-skinny t-t-t-type," who was I to discourage him? I was, in fact, happy to oblige, because my Twiggy types sometimes had so little action that now and again I sort of maneuvered men into "choosing" them.

However, with Stammering Sam there was one big problem. It turned out that on three visits to my house, for all my fixing him up with a skinny girl, he never ever—but never ever—got it up. In other words, he came, but he didn't come. So on the fourth visit I decided to try to put him at ease by teasing him lightly about his performance.

"What's the matter, Sam? Do you like paying money for a soft-on?" I joked.

"N-n-n-no," he said. "I w-w-w-want to get my money's worth, but I don't like s-s-s-skinny w-w-w-w-women."

I was flabbergasted. "But that's what you asked me for the very first time you came here," I pointed out.

"No, I-I-I-I was trying to t-t-t-tell you my wife is s-s-s-s-s-skinny, and I wanted a d-d-d-different kind."

I felt so guilty and embarrassed that I looked for the fattest woman in the place, who turned out to be my maid. She was an older woman, but she had a terrific fat ass and huge tits, and I paid her ten dollars out of my own pocket to fuck him, which she did. She straddled him first, then smothered him all over with her hot, zaftig flesh. Afterward, he came out smiling all over his face and said, "T-t-t-t-that was the b-b-b-best f-f-f-fuck I've ever had."

The immoral of that story is, if you're going to spend money in a whorehouse, you should expect value and tell the madam what you want in advance. No madam alive is going to offer a refund once a customer has had his turn. That would be like getting an airline to return the price of the ticket after the trip was over, just because the passenger didn't dig the stewardess. Not only that, but until they legalize brothels, you can't complain to Ralph Nader or the Better Business Bureau, which would then be called the Better Monkey Business Bureau.

So the first rule of making cocksure you're well spent in a whorehouse is to make your preferences known. You wouldn't go to the local bar and ask for a lemonade when you were thirsting for a bourbon, any more than you should visit a brothel and settle for a lanky redhead when you were horny for a plump brunette. You obviously don't reject a girl in her presence, but you call the madam aside and say, "May I speak with you alone for a moment?" But sometimes men are so sheepish they won't ask outright for a particular girl, in which case the madam may recommend a girl simply because she hasn't done much work that evening, while another girl who has the face of Brigitte Bardot and the body of Raquel Welch has been shuttled out to the kitchen and sits there filing her nails. The internal code of the whorehouse is that everybody should get an equal amount of work and an equal share of the spoils, to the maximum extent possible. That's fine for the girls, but you really don't have to let it be at your expense if you have enough gumption to speak up in advance. *You're* the customer.

The girls are usually cooperative, but they're also human. If the raving beauty of the establishment happens to walk into the living room and the customer immediately picks her, ignoring a girl he was just about to carry off and make his own, it will quite often upset the other girls to such a degree that there will be an unpleasant atmosphere. And, as a result, the man will be made uncomfortable in various unsubtle ways. Sometimes, when the girls get jealous of one another, they even start fighting, and they don't care whether there are Johns around or not. Of course, none of this alters the fact that if the customer is being urged to go with a girl he doesn't like and he lets himself be swayed from his preferences, he's obviously not going to get his money's worth, nine times out of ten.

Whether or not a man gets full value in a pay-for-play depends a lot on the type of operation. First of all, on the lowest level, there's the streetwalker, who works corners and doorways on Lexington Avenue or Broadway, if it happens to be in New York, or comparable areas in other cities, and either takes the John back to a nearby fleabag hotel or even fucks him behind the staircase. This may be his special kick, the whole atmosphere of sleaziness, in which case he's getting a good deal. But there are hazards that can easily outweigh the economy. He may have a bigger bill to settle later if her pimp has him rolled for his money, or if she steals his wallet. Then there's the rising cost of penicillin injections for the extra bonus of VD she may have given him.

The second individual worker is more of an "entrepreneur." She's usually a girl who's not that young anymore, who operates as an individual from her own reasonably pleasant apartment in cooperation with a tight-knit group of four or five others. These girls have a steady clientele, which they swap around among themselves; however, the assortment of girls is not always that entrancing, and sometimes the man feels he might just as well have stayed home. The independent call girl is another laborer in the vineyard who works for herself. Usually she operates up-scale in fairly classy surroundings and is more of an expensive part-time mistress than anything else.

In a more organized situation, you have the houses that operate on several levels, ranging from El

Cheapo to all-creature-comforts, and the difference between one end of the spectrum and the other is the difference between eating at a truck-stop diner and supping at "21." In the first kind of establishment, the man may pay from fifteen to twenty-five dollars in a place where the madam virtually pushes him in and out of the door as quickly as possible. If he hasn't had it in fifteen minutes, she's quite capable of pounding on the door and telling him to haul his ass out of there *tout de suite*. It's all a question of economics. When you pay a low price, you're not going to get an hour of a girl's time, because, quite simply, in these inflationary days, neither she nor the madam would make much of a living out of it.

The next step up offers reasonably tolerable surroundings, tempered by the turnstile approach. A typical example is found in the lower levels of Las Vegas, where a customer pays his money and never even sees the madam, and where the whole ambience, while not unpleasant, is more like an automobile assembly line than a house of pleasure. Then there's the high-class brothel, where the madam calls the shots, supervises the action, and does as much as possible to ensure that the customer gets what he paid for and that he wants to come back again and again. Another thing that's carefully observed in a house such as this is the rotating of girls and the frequent change of faces. A man wants variety, and variety is supposed to be one of the chief attractions of a brothel.

Generally, a top-drawer madam will charge you between fifty and a hundred dollars a shot, and that means if you're not through in two minutes the girl won't rush you out. But she's not going to spend an hour with you, either. However, if a girl from a house goes over to a man's hotel—that's "take-out" cuisine—she has a drink first and stays a minimum of an hour, during which time he can just talk to her (if he's a little nuts) or make love, and then maybe sit and chat for a while afterward. This is one way of getting more for your money in terms of the girl's company. But remember that in a "take-out" situation, while the man's entitled to be with the girl for an hour, he can still come only once for the same fee. Generally speaking—and I'm talking about ninety-nine situations out of a hundred—the girl prefers the man to get down to the action right away. And after a minimum of "conversation," she wants to get up, get dressed, and get the hell out of there.

One man who is definitely not going to get his money's worth in a whorehouse is the premature ejaculator. I had a customer in New York who was a forty-year-old nervous businessman who had never been to a brothel before. I decided to take care of him myself. He had a back problem, he said, having suffered a slipped disk, so I agreed to give him a nice back rub before we got started making love. We undressed, and I asked him to lie face-down on my pale blue satin sheets. Soon he began sliding his body up and down while I was rubbing his back and shoulders with lotion. Little by little, I proceeded with my fingers toward his rear end; then I inserted one of them until it sort of touched his prostate gland, and—bingo!—he came then and there without actually having touched me. This was very similar to the case of the college boy who came to interview me and, instead, came all over my black satin sheets. In this instance, however, the man was hardly in a position to be able to blame it on his callow youth.

Maybe it was my fault, in a way. I frankly doubt that he would have come without my touching his prostate. He was much too meek to complain, but even if he had objected to getting figuratively screwed because he had shot his wad without being literally screwed, I wouldn't have given him the time of day, let alone handed his money back. After all, I had given him my time, not to mention the cost of having my bedsheets cleaned.

This man was hardly the Lone Ranger. Many customers are so nervous, or so horny, when they reach a hooker's apartment that they go straight to the bathroom, then jump into bed, and immediately on inserting the penis into her vagina, shoot their load. If a man wants to prevent premature ejaculation and get value for his money, he'll either masturbate before coming there or concentrate on last week's football game until he's ready to switch to the matter at hand and let nature take its course.

There are certain men, usually younger customers between the ages of twenty-five and thirty-five, who have learned to control the problem of premature ejaculation they may have had in their teens and have developed a pretty good technique. If they also happen to be good-looking, then in their view this happy combination automatically qualifies them as God's gift to women. They pay twenty-five dollars or fifty dollars, depending on the whorehouse, and they demand a full hour's session. These men think fifty dollars entitles them to do anything they want. They'll want to try every variation of lovemaking—eating the girl, making her eat them, putting it in her ear, her armpit, or her rear end. Then they want to come three times, which is not fair and not permitted. To get around this, they hold back as if they had a dildo there instead of a penis composed of human flesh, and they'll keep on fucking and fucking for a full hour. This is the kind of client hookers despise most of all. And certainly, if a man just wants to prove he's a good lover in order to massage his own ego, half an hour should be more than enough to establish that historic point.

Another kind of client is the man who's angry with himself for coming too soon and who wants to squeeze in a second shot. He has twenty different positions in mind and is so busy concentrating on position number five, instead of on holding back, that he loses control and ejaculates all over the place. In this case the girl is definitely not going to give him an extra treat. The man might complain that he didn't get his money's worth. Maybe he didn't, but he's not going to get a freebie, either.

Not every customer is a boor; indeed, far from it. Some men are not only good lovers but also nice people. These are the ones with whom a girl will really enjoy making love—for half an hour or so. Nevertheless, there's often a certain degree of faithfulness in these situations on both sides. Some madams are quite proud that they have regular customers who keep coming back and asking for the same girl. But even the regulars relish a change of pace and face, and usually the madam is shrewd enough to see to it that, every once in a while, Old Faithful is unavailable.

One type of man who will definitely not get what he paid for in a brothel is the drunk, and of course it's nobody's fault but his own. One effect a lot of alcohol has on the penis is that, if the man is lucky enough to get an erection in the first place, he'll just keep pumping away for half an hour. It's a losing battle, because he won't be able to come, no way. In that case, the girl is entitled to say, "That's it! You've had your turn." In his mind, he didn't get sexual satisfaction because he didn't get his rocks off, but he should have thought of this when he was having one too many on another kind of rocks.

Then there's the drunk who can't even get a hard-on to begin with; in fact, if he's really tied one on, he may just fall asleep on the nest. Madams, in New York at least, see this sort of thing at its worst on St. Patrick's Day, when every whorehouse in town is filled with drunken Irishmen (God save them), all very rowdy and very demanding and very ineffective for all their huffing and puffing. They screw the girls to pieces and can't come, but never think to blame themselves. Then again, St. Patrick's Day comes but once a year, thank the Lord, so I guess we can stand it.

A package deal is a good way of getting a break in a brothel. Let's say a stag party of twelve bachelors arranges to take over a house, and there are only four bedrooms. A madam might decide to pair them up, two guys taking a king-size bed with two girls. Strictly speaking, while they are entitled to come only once per couple, they may swap girls and get away with a bit of pleasant cheating on the side. After all, the madam is getting double profit out of a single room.

In general, a hooker depends on and responds to the prevailing atmosphere in the whorehouse. If, for example, there's a gang-bang party with twelve noisy guys drinking and running around naked with big erections, she may want to get it all over and done with as quickly as possible. However, sometimes one of those twelve revelers happens to be a really nice guy. In that case, something very pleasant might develop while the two of them are alone in the bedroom. Usually, men in crowd scenes like that are young and attractive, and the girl might decide to give him a wonderful time because she happens to be taken with that particular John.

In general, when a man goes to a hooker on an impulse, it's because he suddenly feels horny at the office, on the street, or in a bar. He usually calls and wants to see her in half an hour. A clever hooker never turns down a client or says, "I'm rather busy right now, why don't you come by in three hours?" Right now is when he feels the urge; in three hours he might lose both his impulse and his hard-on—or find another brothel.

A lot of men think a hooker is just a warm hole to stick a penis into, and those men will probably get just that—one, two, three, bam, bam, in and out. In fact, with most streetwalkers and El Cheapo houses, many girls can be nasty and brittle. But in a good house, with a steady high-class clientele, a girl can feel sympathetic to a person who is nice, and she'll be kinder and won't rush him as much. Hookers can be quite understanding listeners, which is one reason, believe it or not, many men go and pay their money at a whorehouse. The problems men bring to the hooker are often nonsexual. But one thing she isn't interested in hearing is the complaints of a married man. I mean, a man too often accuses his wife of not understanding or loving him, or of just not knowing how to fuck (or suck), when all the time it is he who needs to be taught a lesson.

Then too, a lot of men feel awfully guilty about going to a house of prostitution. Incredible as it seems, they are likely to produce pictures of the wife and kids. For some strange reason, this makes them feel less guilty, when you'd think it would be just the opposite. Hookers generally don't mind this at all. As a madam, I've found it interesting and have spent hours discussing a man's life and personal problems, provided I like him as a person. This, of course, is another special service of a whorehouse. We have no claim on a man, so we can't object to his introducing his wife and kids into the conversation. But if a man tried that with a new acquaintance whom he is seriously interested in having an affair with, she'd soon tell him to get lost.

Guilt is one thing, hang-ups are another. Men who bring their hang-ups to a whorehouse—not the kooks, but the men with an inferiority complex or a bruised ego—are usually prepared to pay up. Impotent men, and I mean completely impotent, were among the biggest spenders I had in my house, because they would pay anything and do anything to assuage their masculine ego. They'd become experts in oral sex, the use of vibrators or dildoes, or encourage all kinds of lesbian scenes between the girls—whatever they thought would make the girls happy.

It's the same for a man with an undersized penis; he'll do anything to distract your attention from it. Many of these men ask a hooker, "What does it feel like?" even though they must assume a hooker fakes quite often. They say, "Am I big enough for you? Am I hard enough? Did I come too quick for you? Honey, I want you to have four orgasms." These men need this kind of reassurance, because maybe their wives tell them, "Oh, not tonight, I have a headache." So they're pretty downbeat, and their egos are so starved that a good hooker need say only, "Oh, honey, you're fantastic. I came so suddenly!" That's exactly what he wants to hear. A stiff cock doesn't know when it's being put on. This, by the way, is why a hooker has to get her money up front, because when a man is horny, he'll pay as much as he can spare. Afterward, it's all promises, promises.

One economy a man can effect is the clever timing of his visits to a brothel. If he gets stiff when business is usually slack, say around lunchtime or on a quiet afternoon, quite often the girls and the madam are happy to have a man walk in and just relax. If he's a nice guy, they'll buy him drinks, sit and talk, and spend a lot more time with him. As for the madam herself, if the John pleases her, not necessarily in the physical sense, but if she approves of him in general, he's going to get better attention and service. Another smart move for the John is to realize that the key to the house is the madam; if the client treats her with respect, maybe even bringing her a gift of flowers or liquor, his satisfaction is just about assured.

So the next time you take your penis to a brothel to give it a big treat, remember that the way to the house beauty's stomach is through the madam's heart. With this in mind, you're sure to get full value—fair fucks for your bucks—and become a "Dear John" in the best sense of the phrase.

CHAPTER THIRTEEN

Exotic Penises I Have Known, OR, Oddballs, Perky Pricks, and Other Strange Bedfellows

I thought I knew all there was to know about the mating habits of the penis until an experience I had in England a few years ago. It was at a weekend party at a country home so stately it made even the White House seem rustic. Everybody there was Lord Somebody-or-Other, or the Duke of What-Not, and there were Rolls-Royces and chauffeurs all over the place. I had been invited by a man I met at Tramps (the super "in" club in London); I called him Bruce Brighteyes because he had the bluest, prettiest eyes you can imagine. He was also elegant, witty, and gorgeous, and I was anticipating a really nice love affair with him.

It was quite a big party, and the people were very friendly; they knew I had just arrived from the States, because my picture had been all over the newspapers, and they were all talking about my book, *The Happy Hooker*. I must say that some of the women struck me as being sort of prim-looking. This impression was confirmed during the weekend, when I managed to get away alone with some of the husbands, several of whom complained that their wives were completely frigid. But the men of the aristocracy are in no position to seek other outlets, because their social world is so small that word gets around very quickly. It's no secret that a few indiscretions have caused political scandals in Britain. And English wives are almost as jealous as American women. I remember one man who told me he was very glad to have me teach him new tricks but that he didn't know quite what to do with them, because his wife would wonder where he learned all these fancy techniques. This reminded me of my brother-in-law in South Africa; I carefully taught him what to do with his cock, and then he complained that he couldn't use his new knowledge on my sister. First, because she was too uptight, and second, because she would guess he had been cheating—and with me, of all people.

As I fucked my way through the male house guests at that weekend party, I started to notice something I subsequently confirmed about Englishmen of that generation and class: at least twenty-five percent of them are sexual masochists. They would reminisce about their schooldays, when a master—or in earlier years, a stern nanny—used to whip them. Most of them expressed a desire for me to oblige them with discipline, a spanking, or worse, preferably while we were naked in bed. It was something they had concealed from their wives, who they felt would not appreciate their kinks. But they knew I'd soon be leaving for Canada and would not be around to tell anyone, and so they felt they could let their hair down.

So much for the aristocracy. I was really looking forward to curling up in bed with my partner, Bruce Brighteyes, and having a *normal* sexual encounter. It would be the first time we had slept together, and I was all juiced up about it. I had been assigned a lovely big room with medieval decor and a snug four-poster oak bed with a canopy over it. Brighteyes tiptoed into my room after everyone was safely asleep, and I welcomed him eagerly.

When we started undressing and I stepped out of my panties, he noticed a chain I was wearing around my waist and became fascinated. "What a pretty chain you have on," he said. "Do you mind if I play with it?" It was a white-gold chain that looked cold and steely. Suddenly he asked me if I would mind tying it around his balls. I was not expecting masochism from him and was sorry to find out he had those tendencies, but I played along. I took his penis in my hand and tied a series of elaborate knots around it and his balls with my chain. He became very excited. Then he asked me to take a length of thin rope (which he just happened to have along) from his jacket pocket, and I did a really good job of tying him to the bedpost.

I had brought with me two whips which I'd bought at the Saddlery, thought I certainly hadn't expected to use them on Brighteyes. When he asked me to hit him a little, I got the whips from my suitcase. One whip was large and made a lot of noise, but its bark was worse than its bite; though the other was smaller, it had a mean little sting to its tail. To freak him out a little, I used the big whip on the bed right next to his face, and he really got conniptions just listening to the swish of the leather. The small one I used on his bottom. He had a big erection but showed no signs of coming. Sometimes men don't come, even though you're acting out their dearest fantasy; they just stay hard until you get them out of the scene. Or sometimes, if you haven't tied their hands, they jerk off while you're beating them or they rub against the bedsheets until they come. (The slave is seldom allowed to fuck.)

Next, Bruce Brighteyes became fascinated with my steel hairbrush, which was sitting within reach on the night table, and he asked me to pat him on his backside with it. Then he wanted me to touch his balls lightly with the steel bristles, and I started softly and carefully, until he begged me to go harder and harder. He kept an erection all the time; in fact, his penis was sort of purple because it was trussed so tight with the rope and chain. I also sucked him, which finally made it sort of exciting for me—I was still hoping we would soon make love together. But then he pleaded for me to start striking his penis and balls quite viciously with the spiky steel. When drops of blood trickled out, he was absolutely ecstatic. I, on the other hand, was not, and I insisted on stopping, because it was becoming too sadistic for me. Besides, by then I realized it was an exercise in futility. I was *not* going to get laid by Bruce Brighteyes—not that night or any other night.

I tell that story to illustrate the incredible amount of punishment a sensitive set of organs like the male genitalia can actually endure. But let's talk now about some of the more pleasant habits, characteristics, and varieties of this most remarkable portion of the human anatomy, the best part of a man. There's no real standard to go by when it comes to the penis. Every one of them is different. And, no, bigger is not necessarily better. The rest of this chapter covers commonly encountered variations in color, size, and shape, as well as some of the more surprising cases I've encountered. The point to bear in mind, however, is that it's what you do with what you've got that counts.

But let's not kid ourselves. Both sexes are preoccupied—sometimes I think "obsessed" is a better word—with size. Okay, let's cater to that obsession for a few pages. How can you tell with his clothes on whether a man is hung like a horse or like a mouse?

Experts claim there is no relationship whatsoever between the size of a man's penis and any other part of his body, but I have found this not to be the case. Based purely on intuition, observation, and experience—and scientific opinion aside—I have been able to gauge the size and general shape of a man's penis by examining the part of his anatomy it resembles most, his hands.

For example, a man with narrow, bony fingers almost always has a longish, thin cock. A man with fleshy butcher's hands has a softer, flabbier cock. A man with big, strong hands and well-shaped fingers is very likely to have a large, handsome penis. And the man with spatulate fingers that have pulpy tips usually has a biggish soft head on his penis.

However, there's also a fail-safe and more accurate method a woman can use to find out how long a man's penis is while he still has his clothes on and before she decides to make him her lover. She takes the middle finger of his right hand, bends it as far forward as it will go and marks the spot where his fingertip rests on the heel of his palm. The distance between that spot and his extended middle fingertip when his hand is open measures almost to the millimeter the length of his cock when erect.

To measure the width, she takes the index finger and adjoining middle finger of his left hand, and keeping them closed against each other, she juxtaposes them with the tightly closed index and middle fingers of the right hand. With the two sets of two fingertips facing each other and all four fingers kept closed, she wraps her thumb and index finger around the man's finger grouping and thus learns precisely how thick his penis is.

All very well, you say, but how is the man going to respond to all this finger manipulation? That's the beauty part. If the woman tells him the purpose of the game, and if he measures up, she's as good as in bed with him. If he doesn't, and if he's a nice guy, she still can have a lot of fun in bed. In other words, it's an ingenious and provocative way for a woman to say, *"Voulez-vous couchez avec moi?"* If she doesn't want to be that direct, or really intends to turn him down unless he stacks up, it isn't too difficult to pretend she's doing it as a measure of character, intelligence, or whatever.

Of course, there's a more direct method of telling with his clothes on, but it isn't very accurate. That is simply taking a good look at the bulge in his pants. If it's prominent, that probably means he does have a big cock and balls, but it also may mean he's caught on to the tricks of male ballet dancers who have been known to gild the lily by rounding out their jockstraps with lamb's wool. Homosexuals on the make have also picked up this stratagem.

This brings me to a suggestion that could make

somebody very rich. Lots of men who are very well equipped fail to give any hint of their endowment because they happen to be hung further back; it's there, but it's not conspicuous underneath all that clothing. Why doesn't somebody invent a brassiere for men's crotches? Not padding, but something supportive. It could be advertised as contributing to crotch comfort—after all, you've seen plenty of men trying to free their balls from the confinement of the stupid trousers they wear—and that would be rationalization enough for introducing this new appliance, which we'll call "The Krotch King."

You don't always need physical clues to know when a guy has a really small one. He's the man in the bar who brags, "Last night I had this beautiful babe, and boy did she rave about my physique." That's your cue to make tracks. The only big thing about a man like this is his mouth. If his tall tales don't turn you off to begin with, finding out that his penis doesn't measure halfway up to them will.

Granted, you don't often overhear a direct statement of that sort. But there are plenty of men who make indirect statements, even without opening their big mouths. This is the sort of chap who throws his money around, wears loud clothes, and most telling of all, has the biggest, flashiest car around. The man who brags the most is the man who compensates the most for what he lacks, whether in size or sexual performance, by wearing his supposed sex appeal like a dunce cap.

Now that we've had our fun posing as cock detectives, let's get back to the subject of the infinite variety of penises that abound in this wonderful world of ours. I happen to be sensitive to color, so I'll start with that.

Coloration is obviously just a matter of aesthetics, for it does not affect a man's performance by one iota—though it may be a psychological turn-on (or turn-off) for a woman. One of the strangest "color schemes" I ever saw was on a Eurasian man (in his case, a mixture of Portuguese and Chinese ancestry) who had an even *café-au-lait* complexion everywhere on his face and body except on the shaft of his penis, which was dappled like a piebald horse, with large pigmented striations of pink and brown. Then I have seen one that was raw pink, except for the abstract-shaped orangish areas from the balls right to the very tip. This man also had an albino streak in his sandy hair, and his eyelashes were completely white, in contrast to his brown eyebrows. That really should have told me what to anticipate on a lower level, although I always expect the unexpected when a man takes off his pants. Generally speaking, the color of the penis conforms to certain facial characteristics. For example, a man with liverish-colored lips and eyelids will usually have a darkish penis, no matter what the facial complexion is. I had an affair with a famous (and married) New York television personality who had a nice light caramel complexion, but his cock was a very funky dark brown with a rosy pink head on it.

There is generally not much difference in coloration between one penis and the next, but if a man is a fair Scandinavian type, you can almost be assured of a wan-colored penis, while redheaded men usually have whitish ones with maybe a sprinkling of freckles and carrot-colored pubic hair. What's unusually stimulating for me is a man with a nice hairy abdomen, no matter what the color, and lots of pubic hair—like a big bush with a lovely tree growing out of it. With certain kinds of browner, swarthier men—for instance, certain Israelis who are Sephardic Jews—I get very turned on to the color of the penis, which is almost Negroid, with a dark purplish base and a pinkish head. Black men have an intriguing color, because the penis is a very dark, coppery brown and sometimes seems to have a shimmery patina; when the foreskin is retracted, it's usually fawny-pink on top. Almost as intriguing to me is a black woman's vagina, which has a gorgeous purply tint.

To me, black is beautiful as far as the penis is concerned. However, it is definitely a myth that black is bigger. This cock-and-bull story got around because, generally speaking, the black penis doesn't shrivel up as much as the white one when the erection goes down. Yes, it does look bigger, but only on the slack. When the black penis grows, it gets hard without growing very much, either in width or length, while the white one can grow to as much as three or four times its slack size. The average white man's cock tends to diminish to as little as two to four inches in length, and even the width gets considerably smaller.

For my taste, the flaccid penis is the least attractive thing on a man's body. That is why I don't get at all turned on by even handsome men at a nudist camp. I might get turned on to a woman's body when she's sunbathing or playing badminton in the nude, because her anatomy, unlike a man's, doesn't advertise its state with a turned-on hard-sell or a turned-off and uninviting soft-on. Her body is alluring either way. But when you see men walking around with sneakers, tennis racket, and a soft-on, it looks ridiculous, except for a few who are lucky enough to own a nice long erect penis.

The penis I like to look at, and touch, and suck, and fuck, is one that has a nice thick shaft (which does not have to be overly long) and a rather large head, so that the prick looks very much like a mushroom. Usually the ring around the glans is the most sensitive part, and somehow it is a tremendous turn-on to suck a man with a big head. Of course, it can create problems, particularly when entering the vagina, because the head can occasionally be almost as big as a fist, and unless the woman is really lubricated, it can be quite painful. What is really important is the size of the head, really more important than the width or length of the shaft. The base can have a soft inch in the middle and since it doesn't make too much physical difference, it's no problem as long as it stands up and does the job. But sometimes the head is so big that it can be top-heavy. I have seen some cases where the shaft was long, thin, and flexible, like the Eiffel Tower, with a very large head, so that, when it grew erect, it would sway back and forth like the aerial on a speeding car. The problem is to keep from laughing and thus spoiling a perfectly good fuck.

I have noticed that Italian men, by and large, have a much bigger head than shaft. I first discovered this when I was about twenty years old and was sleeping with both Dutch and Italian men in Holland. With the

Dutch men, while everything was nice as far as the uniform shape of the shaft was concerned, the penis seemed to end up in the head and didn't broaden out to a nice protruding bulb, whereas the Italian mushrooms were big and exciting.

The appearance of the penis and its size while performing sixty-nine are important. The balls can also be extremely nice for a woman to play around with. In my opinion, the size and shape of a man's balls make absolutely no difference to his capacity as a lover, but from the aesthetic point of view, it is much nicer if a man has two firm, tight balls, and not flabby ones with lots of skin hanging loose. I've seen young men with scrotums that look and feel like empty gunnysacks, and older men who have thin, tight nuts. I once had a handsome fifty-four-year-old lover who has cock and balls stronger and firmer than any twenty-four-year-old. He is into yoga, which may or may not have anything to do with it, but basically I believe he is just a very healthy man.

I have often been asked if exercise can change the size, shape, or condition of the penis and testicles. A team of aerobic exercise specialists at a Midwestern university has been experimenting with exercising mice on a treadmill, and they have observed that the mice's testicles are getting larger and firmer.

Physical exercise is definitely good for sexual health, and you should take that into consideration before indulging in a sudden and unaccustomed binge of sexual acrobatics. One should not overdo the action, unless you exercise regularly, without taking it slowly at first. A man of forty-five who has led a sedentary desk-bound life comes into the brothel and may hardly make it through round one, while another, more athletic and vigorous man ten years older makes out like a virtuoso. Just as you would consult a physician if you were inactive and planning to start an exercise routine, so you should keep a steady pace in your sex life. Remember what happened to two famous swashbuckling actors who were trying to keep up with their reputations as sex symbols. One died on top of a young chick in a hotel room in Canada, and the other breathed his last as he was pumping away at a young blond in a hotel on Gramercy Park in New York.

It is no secret that most, if not all, men are concerned with the size of their penis, but very few have figured out what is average and how to go about accurately measuring it. The average erect penis is about six and a quarter inches along the top surface from the angle at the base to the eye at the top, four inches in circumference, and one and five-eighths inches at the thickest diameter. But a man shouldn't be disappointed if he is smaller, because since this is a universal average, half the men in the world will fall into that category.

I've known men with the world's biggest cocks who were very boring in bed. Some men who have a large penis think they don't have to rely on foreplay or caressing or oral sex because all they've got to do is insert their big prick inside a woman's cunt and that will do the job. Little do they know that they are often too hard, too rough, inconsiderate, and selfish in their lovemaking, and they simply bang the living hell out of the girl and her vagina.

On the other hand, a man with a little pecker can be clever enough with his foreplay to divert my attention with other activities so that when he finally slips it in and has his screw, I come too. I've seen men who were completely unable to get it up or who had such a tiny penis that they learned how to compensate. They come to a whorehouse and all they want is to eat pussy or use vibrators; their main concern is to please the woman. Obviously, the wives involved never seem to be pleased, so the men go to the whorehouse to feed their egos. They've got to hear, "This man gives better head than anybody else—he might not have a bigger cock, but boy can he turn you on!"

A short while ago I met a gorgeous man in Montreal who I thought at first was Eskimo because of his unusual golden skin—what do I know about racial types, I'm just a simple Dutch girl—but I found out he was French-Jewish, and on the face of it, everything a woman could desire. He was handsome, attentive, charming, rich, and unmarried. He invited me to dinner, and afterward we went dancing, and he was very sensitive, touching and kissing me on the neck, ears, shoulders, and hands all evening. I wanted to get up close against him even while we were dancing, but the music was so noisy and fast that it didn't require physical touch, and I had to wait until we went back to my apartment.

When we were finally alone together, he kind of shied away from me, which made me all the more curious, because I really liked him, and he'd gotten me so horny and juicy. We took separate showers, and when I was through I walked into the bedroom, where he was already waiting between my black satin sheets. I turned the lights off, lit a nice perfumed candle, and climbed into bed beside him. That was when I got a terrific shock. I saw that he not only had the penis of a seven-year-old boy but that he would never get it up, no way.

I thought he might have had problems adjusting to the situation, and that was why he was in bed with the Happy Hooker, but he seemed to have no ego problems at all, even though I didn't hide my shock. Then he said, "Look, there are other things we can do besides making love. For that you've got your own boyfriend." I was so horny to have him all night long that, even though he ate me beautifully, I tried and tried to suck it up even a little. But my hardest was his softest, and the night was a big—or little—zero. His balls were tiny too, and even if his penis had managed to stand up, it would have been no bigger than my middle finger. Needless to say, I realized then why such a good-looking man had never married or had any steady girlfriends.

That was the smallest I ever encountered in bed, but I've actually seen even smaller cocks. I once went out on a luxury yacht in California with a Chinese tycoon who wanted to be buddies with me. At one point we anchored and dived into the sea for a swim. When we came back on board and he took off his swimming trunks to get dressed, I saw that he had the most minuscule penis you could ever hope not to see. It was so small it was all but inverted. It looked like a rosebud or a nipple, and I'm sure that, while you're usually surprised at just how big a small prick can grow in erection, his cock eventually would have come to no more than my pinkie. However, I avoided doing any further research in this particular case.

Then there's the so-called royal pencil case, the one that never advanced beyond boyhood size because of generations of inbreeding. This famous royal lover was known to be afflicted with sexual insecurity over the inadequacy of the pencil case he'd inherited. When he met a certain divorcée who was able to put him at his ease and somehow assure him it did not matter, he ran off with her. To make it more binding, the woman had mastered the art of voluntary vaginal control, so all was well that ended well.

Sometimes it doesn't end well, as in the tragic case of Paul Bern, the Hollywood producer who married the reigning sex goddess of the thirties, Jean Harlow. He became so depressed on his wedding night that he brutally beat her black and blue, and later killed himself by trying to hack off his own tiny genitals.

Men who feel they were short-changed when penises were handed out will be gratified to know there are big problems associated with overendowment. I know a Dutchman who is acutely embarrassed about the enormous size of his penis. He has had numerous girls, particularly those with small vaginas, who bled slightly after they made love with him, as gentle as he tried to be. The width of his penis was extraordinary and was outclassed only by the size of the head. Moreover, when he put his pants on, he had to fold his penis backward and sit on it—he said it was more comfortable than having it hang left or right, the normal way for men to "dress"—so that it wouldn't pop up in his jeans.

Some men are celebrated for their supercocks, such as the late Latin diplomat playboy whose reputation, like his penis, deservedly went before him. There is a country-and-western singer whose penis is said to be so large that he outdistanced his horse. Possibly the most famous penis of modern times belonged to "Superman" (he even wore a cloak with an "S" symbol on it), a character who used to hang out in the San Francisco brothel in Havana at the height of its decadence in the mid-1950's. His penis measured twelve inches on the slack and had a head as big as a drinking goblet. Horny ladies from all over the world were wild about it, and wealthy women paid him lots of money for just an hour of his time. He would have to insert his penis while it was still practically limp, as it would be far too painful for most women when it was erect.

As far as I can learn, the longest penis on medical record was one that measured fourteen inches in its detumescent—or flaccid—state. In this man's case, doctors had to advise the man to insert a small sponge in his wife's vagina to protect her uterus from a dangerous pounding during intercourse. The glans, the pulpy head of the penis, was designed by nature to be a natural cushion. But in rare cases, like this one, it does not afford sufficient protection.

The male genital organs, the penis and the scrotum, are a marvel of anatomical engineering. The scrotum—otherwise known as the balls, gonads, testicles, *cojones,* or nuts—is located between the penis and the perineum (the sensitive little bridge between the anus and the balls) and is made up of a pouch of dark, wrinkled skin, lightly covered with longish hairs and "pimpled" with lots of sebaceous glands. Inside the scrotal sac are two testicles, separated by a membrane that can be seen on the outside as a sort of seam running along the middle. The testicles are formed in the abdomen before birth and drop into the scrotum in normal cases. However, nature is not infallible, and sometimes the child suffers from what is known as "undescended testes" and has to have them surgically released before he gets too much older. If one ball descends, however, he can do plenty of damage with that. I have seen four men who had only one ball (apiece), and they did just fine. Often these men are concerned as to whether or not they can produce babies as easily as they could with two balls, but usually there is no problem. It's like a girl with one ovary; she can still get pregnant.

When both balls are removed, it is called castration. Less than a century ago, Vatican choirboys were still routinely castrated, or "emasculated," so they would retain their soprano voices. Eunuchs are another disappearing breed of castrati, or de-balled men. Although castrati cannot produce babies, if their emasculation took place post-puberty, modern hormone therapy can give them back their masculine characteristics, such as a deep voice and body and facial hair.

There is another situation in which the testicles are unnatural. That is the case of the hermaphrodite, who is a person born with both testes and ovaries. A friend of mine, who was a musician and boozed so much he didn't always know what he was doing, went home one night with a groupie whom he chose because of her beautiful knockers and sexy face. As they were going to his hotel room, the girl started crying and said, "I really don't think I can go to bed with you." This was confusing, because she had been so crazy about him at the rock concert, but he coaxed her into his room anyway. While he was washing up, she jumped into the bed and covered herself, but as soon as he jumped in beside her, he found out why she was upset.

He saw that there was a miniature flaccid penis with tiny balls attached. Being as drunk as he was, he didn't say anything but just flicked the little thing away and got inside and fucked her. He doesn't even know if it was a cunt or an ass, but he did say she was one of the horniest girls he had ever met. I suppose she felt she had to try harder. Later she told him he was the first man she had balled in five months, because men would run screaming from the room and call her a freak. She later had a sex-change operation and became a transsexual, but the penis never got hard and "she" never has achieved an orgasm.

The testicles, or nuts, are shaped like large almonds and feel small and soft until maturity, when testosterone secretion promotes growth and makes them rubbery and firm. They are extremely sensitive to the touch, and you can make a man almost vomit with pain by applying hard or sudden pressure. (This is why women are advised to kick rapists in the balls to save themselves.)

Some men claim they can forecast rain because their balls start to itch, and I have found out there is some truth to this. Cold or damp weather causes special muscles to draw the testes to the top of the scrotum as a kind of temperature control. It is important for healthy sperm production that the testicles dangle in the air at a temperature lower than that of the rest of the body, and nature ensures this through her clever ventilation system. For this reason, doctors say that men who wear tight underpants may be jeopardizing their fertility. Dr. Ann Chandley, a genetics researcher at Edinburgh's Western General Hospital, believes that civilized man's tight underpants cause high temperatures in the testicles and are responsible for the fact that his sperm is only seventy-five percent effective, as opposed to ninety-eight percent for a gorilla. She is currently conducting tests with kilted Scotsmen to corroborate her theory.

Sperm is produced in the testicles at the rate of about twenty-five million per gonad per day in normally functioning men, and are nudged out of the manufacturing tubules by the pressures of new ones into a storehouse beside the balls. They can stay alive for two months, and if not used, they just liquefy. On their journey into the world they go up the tubes known as the vas deferens, which ends up at the base of the urinary bladder in structures called the left and right seminal vesicles. These are two-inch-long sacs which produce a yellowish fluid that, in orgasms, forms most of the ejaculate. The vas deferens are the tubes that are surgically severed in the "Band-Aid" birth-control operation known as vasectomy.

The two seminal vesticles penetrate the prostate gland just below the bladder, and open into the urethra, through which the male both urinates and ejaculates. A little sphincter closes off the bladder opening so that, when he comes, the ejaculate won't back up into the bladder. This is why a man cannot pee when he has an erection.

Sometimes the mechanism goes haywire (if, for example, the man is on certain drugs), and his ejaculate seeps or runs into his bladder. This can also happen if you apply pressure to the base of the penis on the underside so that the semen cannot escape through the head, and instead shoots back into the bladder. This is sometimes used as an "unsafe" method of contraception, known as coitus obstructus. The prostate gland itself reaches the size of a walnut in a full-grown male, but for reasons unclear to doctors, it can often become infected and enlarged after age thirty. This is called prostatitis, and since the painful swelling can obstruct his peeing, the gland has to be removed. The prostate gland also secretes a fluid that kills bacteria, and this is why men suffer less from urethral infection, or urethritis, than women.

The penis itself is also known as the joint, dick, cock, prick (Shakespeare first gave it this name), tool, phallus, family jewels, pecker, one-eyed monster, schlong, peter, and one-eyed trouser snake. It is made up of three cylinders, two above and one below, and all are covered at the end with a sensitive pink cap known as the glans, which is the most erotically responsive part of a man's entire body. The cylinder at the underside of the penis is called corpus spongiosum and contains the urethra, for releasing ejaculate and urine. The cylinder also has, at the base, the strong muscles that create the exciting pulsations during his orgasm as they eject the semen in rhythmic contractions at eight-second intervals. The dorsal cylinders, or those on top, are called corpora cavernosa, and they control the hard-on.

When the penis is limp, blood circulates through a complex and ingenious network of blood vessels. But when a man becomes sexually excited, the vessels open and become congested with blood, which is prevented from withdrawing by special valves in the penis veins. When a man's penis is stiff, it is known as the tumescent state.

There are countless irregularities that can show up in the best part of a man. I knew of one young man who became very excited when his penis started staying erect longer and growing a little bigger, because he thought he was on to something. However, he became alarmed when it started getting discolored, hard, and throbbing, and when he realized that all sexual feeling was absent despite his hard-on and it became painful to fuck. He finally took his penis to his doctor, who diagnosed the problem as priapism, which is an erection that simply won't go away. Priapism is quite a serious condition and can cause sterility if not treated soon enough by a doctor. It is caused by a permanent state of blood engorgement in the penis. Some people confuse this with a different condition known as satyriasis, which is a condition in which a man has an excessively frequent hard-on because he feels horny. Satyriasis is also sometimes called male nymphomania.

But for all those men with slight irregularities who have probably exaggerated them out of proportion in their minds, just remember, it could be worse:

Here is the story of Clarence Cool
Who was born with a spiral tool;
He spent his life in fruitless hunt
To find a girl with a corkscrew cunt;
But when he found her he almost dropped dead
'Cause she was born with a left-hand thread.

CHAPTER FOURTEEN

Keep It Clean as a Whistle OR, It Won't Get Blown

I could tell by her worried expression that the pretty dark-haired woman wanted to talk to me but couldn't summon the courage. The ten couples at the rather conservative Easter-weekend party had kept the conversation casual and polite so far, and not at all about sex. But I knew there was something on her mind.

So I smiled at her, and sure enough, she said, "I'm sorry to trouble you, but could I please talk with you for a moment, alone?" She looked uncomfortably toward her husband, an overweight, slightly slovenly man. She was embarrassed to talk in front of him, and I thought I could guess why. It concerned him.

In the next room there was a Ping-Pong table, so I said, "Okay, let's pretend we're going to play a game of table tennis, and you can tell me your problem."

She looked surprised. "How do you know I have a problem?" she said.

"I can tell, and I think I also know what it is."

A frown crossed her face. "How can you know, when I haven't said a word?"

"Your husband is not circumcised," I said, "and he's not too clean, and you like oral sex." She looked at me as if I were a witch. But I really didn't need a crystal ball. He had dirty fingernails, and his reddish hair was kind of greasy; to me that's a sign a man neglects his whole body.

"Yes, that's exactly it," she said. "But how in the world did you know that?" She was really relieved that she didn't have to explain it.

"Because you look like a woman who enjoys sex in every shape and form. You look sensual, but your husband just doesn't look too tidy to me. Since he's a typical WASP, I assume he's not circumcised."

Then she came out of her shell, and she was quite animated. "Yes," she said, "and I like him going down on me, and he wants me to do it to him, but I just feel like gagging when I do. I have two lovely kids, and I love my husband, and I don't want to go to bed with another man. But how can I tell him? What can I do?"

"Give him my books to read."

"No," she said, "he says he knows it all and doesn't need them."

"Then there's only one way to let him know. You have to teach him without telling him he has anything to learn."

Later on, I'll tell you what I told her. But first, some general thoughts about sexual hygiene.

In situations like this, obviously, you have to use tact and discretion. You can't just do what Empress Catherine of Russia did with her legion of lovers. Before the man of her choice (who always had to be tall, handsome, and young) was sent for a performance rating to one of her two most trusted ladies-in-waiting, Countess Bruce or Princess Protassov, who were known as "the testers," the man had to submit to a genital examination by the Scottish physician retained for that purpose. If any of the young men resented being examined for venereal disease, there's no record of his having expressed that resentment out loud.

That technique works fine for an empress, but it's a bit impractical for the rest of us. We don't have to worry too often about VD if we select our partners wisely, but we do have to concern ourselves frequently with plain ordinary cleanliness. And you can't just say, "Boy, you stink!" Nevertheless, that comes pretty close to what I once did at an elegant party in London, where men don't seem to bathe as much as they do here. It was a glittering social event with many wealthy and influential people, many of them chauffeured to the place in their Rolls-Royces or Bentleys.

I noticed one pretty famous actor, a gorgeous hunk of man, well-dressed and well-kempt, who had been trying to get near me all night. This was his first chance. But when I stood next to him, I almost fainted, he had such a pronounced body odor. So I said to him, "Honey, with all the money you have to spend on your chauffeur and Rolls-Royce, why don't you spend a few pence and buy yourself some deodorant?"

He looked flabbergasted, and he said, "Where do you come off, talking to me like this?"

I said, "Well, if you want to have a chance at going to bed with me, forget about it. If you smell that bad under the arms, I'd hate to think about the rest of you."

He turned abruptly away and ignored me. But a

girl who overheard said, "You really zonked it to him!" He was a well-known ladies' man, and she obviously had slept with him. "But you're right, he could use a daily shower. And there's something fishy about his penis—the way it smells."

With all their money and good manners, I don't know why Englishmen of the aristocracy don't like to bathe regularly. Perhaps it's a habit held over from the days when there weren't too many bathrooms. In Europe, generally, people bathe infrequently.

At the same London party, I met ex-call girl Christine Keeler, who was involved in the Profumo scandal that almost brought down the British government, and she too could have used a spot of deodorant. I remember vividly that she had big perspiration stains under her arms and hairy armpits, which I never expected of her.

I realize some men like hair under the arms. In *The Joy of Sex,* the author, who is English, describes underarm hair as "sexy" and shaving it as "vandalism." The Spanish and Italians get turned on by hairy legs and underarms and also like larger, woollier vaginas, while American men prefer smaller, neater ones. And while Linda Lovelace shaved hers completely nude for *Deep Throat,* I don't think bald pussies are exciting for most men. In the Far East, where they are called "white tigers," they're considered downright unlucky for the man whose penis penetrates them.

While hygiene, to me, is one of the most important basics in lovemaking, second only to being able to rise to the occasion, some people believe there's such a thing as being too clean. I think it's necessary to distinguish between fragrance, aroma, and odor. The first is the gilded lily. If a man or woman wants to use a genital spray, that's a matter of personal preference. I've seen men's sprays in sex shops in all kinds of flavors, including banana, strawberry, and chocolate. But these are, hopefully, just for sexual enhancement, and not for hygiene.

I think women's sprays have a nice scent too, but fragrance should be used on top of a clean or natural body aroma, not as an attempt to disguise an odor. That only makes it worse. There's a saying that an erect penis has no conscience, but I always say it has no sense of smell, either. Not being squeaky clean for your lover may not be so serious if he or she doesn't want to perform oral sex on you. It may be that you haven't had a chance to shower after a busy day in the office, it might be the first lay in the morning (the "morning glory"), and you don't feel as fresh as you would like to be after last night's lovemaking, or it may be just an impromptu encounter. In such a situation, there are ways to turn your lover off oral sex gently. He: "Not just now, honey, I want to put it into your lovely pussy." She: "I would love to have you inside me right now with your beautiful strong cock."

When I operated my brothel in New York, I rarely came across men who complained that the girls were not clean enough. After all, we made a fetish of personal hygiene. It was almost always the men who were not that particular about their own bodies. I'd find out, because the girl would come to me and complain.

There's something else about a man's genital odor that few are aware of. It's the scent of their semen.

The way it tastes or smells can depend a lot on what they eat or drink. If a man eats spicy food or drinks a lot of alcohol, it tastes unpleasant and sometimes even bitter. But if he drinks a lot of fruit juices and eats sweet things like caramels, creamy pastries, and chocolates, the semen won't taste like chocolate, of course, but it will taste nicer and more delicate. I used to joke with a former boyfriend whenever we would spend a long summer weekend together. "Darling," I'd say, "eat lots of delicious peaches and nectarines and drink fruit juices so it will go right down to your groin."

Now, let's get back to the woman who asked my advice at the Easter party. First, I had to tell her how to teach her untidy husband the basics of outer cleanliness without offending him. "The next time the kids are tucked away in bed and you have a free evening together, here's what you should do. Create a romantic atmosphere in the bathroom with candlelight, perhaps a radio with some nice music playing, and maybe a glass of champagne. Then run a big warm tub full of water and drop in some fragrant bath oils or frothy bubble bath. Work him into a romantic mood; tell him you have a different treat for him tonight and entice him into the bath."

A sidelight: during the height of the energy crisis in England, they actually had a national advertising campaign that was based on this notion. "Put a bit of romance into your bath by sharing the water. You will be amazed at how much gas you will save." The more staid regarded it as kinky, and a Conservative member of Parliament, John Stokes, called the ad "deplorably vulgar." Another M.P. said, "It's debasing the standard of the Gas Board to suggest we share our baths." But what they didn't understand was that, while trying to save a watt, they could also have been saving a marriage.

"Once you've lured your man into the bath," I told the worried wife, "sit facing each other and make sure you have a big chunk of soap that foams well, and start rubbing each other all over. You will probably have to take the initiative, but I assure you he'll soon be encouraged to join in.

"Start soaping his underarms and chest, then work sensuously down toward his penis. While you gently rub his foreskin with soapy hands—being careful to act not like a mother scrubbing a rebellious child but a woman full of a sense of discovery about her man—he will definitely get an erection. It's up to you whether you let him continue on to orgasm there and then or subtly distract his attention to save it for later. In either case, he'll be squeaky clean."

Obviously, none of this is original with me. A famous New York courtesan, for example, was once quite celebrated for her bathtime specialties in her Long Island mansion. She obviously had more lavish surroundings and props than the average hausfrau, but the end result was basically the same. However, there's a lesson in this. Add a touch of class to the scrubbing operation, and even the most sensitive man will accept it with good grace.

To continue with my advice to the young woman, I said, "Gently insert a soapy finger in his anus and excite him all over again that way. Once more, he can easily reach orgasm; it's up to you to hold off if you want. But make sure he's perfectly clean in case you want to perform around-the-world, or analingus. Then go down to his toes. Toes are phallic in erotic situations, and you can give him a nice toe-job."

Another tub technique, by the way, is to suggestively lick a man's big toes a little and then put one of them into your mouth for just a moment, with the obvious promise of more of everything to come when you get out of the bath and into bed. Still another great position in the bathtub is having the woman stand above her man and sort of lean against him; he then stretches up and kisses her on the vagina. Meanwhile, she can stimulate his balls with her toes. As you can see, there's no limit to one's ingenuity. The alternative is sex by rote, and when that happens, the marriage or other relationship palls.

Getting back to my party acquaintance: "When you step out of the bath, you should both be in a very horny mood," I went on to explain. "So wrap a big fleecy towel around each other and go into the bedroom. Then gently go down on him without his having to insist—or even ask—and say, 'I really love the clean smell of the soap. And you taste so good.' Pretty soon he'll get the message, and you will have converted your husband into Mr. Clean. And you'll both love it."

A few weeks later the woman called me up. Everything went better than she had dared hope. She was absolutely delighted. And so was I. It was a clean story—with a happy ending.

CHAPTER FIFTEEN

My Life and Soft Times, OR, The Reluctant Penis

I had a little Chinese masseuse in New York who would come by when things were quiet to give me a relaxing rub. She was about the only straight person who came through those doors. She knew my house was not exactly a home, but she just did her job, took her fee, and left. One afternoon she arrived quite upset because she thought her previous client had taken her for a "bad type." She complained, "Miss Xaviera, my last customer, he was at six o'clock." She looked very angry. "Who does he think he is? I told him only at six-thirty."

I had no idea what she was talking about, because it was only four in the afternoon. "What's the problem?" I said. "Just go back there at six-thirty."

"No, no, you don't understand," she said. "With this kind of man it's always six o'clock." It may have been Oriental logic, I thought, but it sounded more like a Chinese puzzle. "Six o'clock," she repeated, slipping her hand under the bedsheets and lifting them back. She had stiffened her middle finger, looking sort of embarrassed. Then she relaxed her finger and said, "This is six-thirty." Then I got the point, literally. The man had been lying in bed waiting for her with a hard-on, and that was the Chinese slang way of describing it.

We had a similar hand signal in the brothel to indicate the angle of a man's penis to his body, but this was for the different stages of his life, and was also based on "hard" medical fact. You hold your hand forward, with the palm perpendicular to the floor; the fingers are fanned out, and the thumb is pointing up. The position of the thumb is where his erection stands at age twenty, the index finger is for age thirty, middle finger age forty, second to last finger is where his erection stands at age fifty, and the pinkie is where it ends up around age sixty. And therein lies the cause of so much unnecessary grief—so many men think that because their penis doesn't stand up as high as it once did, they are now threatened with not getting it up at all. But any urologist (cock doctor) can tell them that just because a man's penis doesn't get as high an erection when a man gets older (nor does it go up as fast), that's no reason to start worrying about impotence.

It's all a matter of relativity. It takes three to eight seconds to achieve erection for a man under forty. So what? What's a few minutes more or less in anybody's life? And what real difference does the "angle of inclination" make? It's the *man's* inclination that counts most.

True, a young man can easily be aroused by thoughts, fantasies, and visual sex stimulants, such as seeing a naked woman, reading a dirty book, or even watching two dogs coupling. After forty, the spirit can be just as willing, but the body is not as quick to respond, and it takes more time to get it up. Sometimes direct genital stimulation is required. The great danger is that suddenly the older man says to himself, "Damnit, I must be getting old and impotent." And his wife might even fall into the same trap and accuse him of not finding her attractive anymore because he doesn't get stiff the instant she undresses. Between the two of them they can easily panic and eventually work up to a case of genuine impotence.

Chronic impotence, however, is something else again. Not being able to get it up at all is not directly related to age. Sex therapists say impotence is the single biggest problem brought to them these days; and what is more, it affects an increasing number of younger men.

As the Happy Hooker and the Merry Madam, I've seen many strange and sad sights, but strangest and saddest of all is the sight of man's noblest member lying limp as a dishrag in the midst of a garden of fleshly delights, of beckoning breasts and pulsating pussies. These Knights of the Woeful Whangdoodle are often the most virile of men; they come from every class, every nationality, every age group. The point to be remembered and emphasized is that *every* man, no matter how old he is, has at some time in his sex life had the experience of not being able to get a hard-on, or else losing it before he enters the woman or before he finishes screwing. This is by no means an abnormal condition. A man with a reasonably secure ego can take it in his stride and shrug it off; but a more vulnerable man makes it a self-fulfilling prophecy.

I recently went to a party in Toronto with some fairly well-known playboys who were all married men having a wifeless night out. They were all really looking forward to having me there, treated me like a celebrity, and we all flirted around and danced together. The man I was most attracted to was a handsome guy who was thirty-two years old and the father of three kids. When it came time to use one of the available rooms, we more or less understood we would disappear together. We went upstairs, took showers, and went into the bedroom, where I softened the lights and started sweet-talking in his ear and kissing him. I thought I was being quite exciting to him, but when I reached down with my hand, I discovered his penis was not hard at all. So I rubbed it, and it got up a tiny bit, but not much. I said, "Honey, what's wrong?"

He said, "Xaviera, I don't know. I've looked forward to this so much, to being in bed with the Happy Hooker. I just feel sort of strange."

I tried to reassure him. "Don't worry," I said. "It'll all come out all right."

And he said, "Tell me, how many men have you slept with?"

I said, jokingly, "You mean this afternoon?" Obviously, I wasn't a hooker anymore, so I don't know why he asked me that question. Nevertheless, I decided to answer him. "About three thousand men, at least," I said. At that point, what little hard-on he had went right down the drain.

I didn't think his ego would get crushed that quickly. But since I had felt half a hard-on, I thought there might be something there, so I moved down and sucked and sucked until I had a sore jaw. After about half an hour, it did get a little larger and harder, though not really stiff, so I took the female dominating position and crawled on top of him. But just as I was about to insert it, he said, "Oh, you must be so fantastic—you know all those terrific positions, and I suppose you expect the man to keep up with you." Immediately, his erection, which had taken me half an hour to get up, went down again. I've heard that, at times, when a man is with a celebrated female sex symbol, he becomes temporarily impotent because he thinks the woman will be too much for him, but this was the first time it had happened to me.

By now I was becoming a bit bored with this playboy and his immature ego, but my own ego demanded I get him to come. So I told him to pretend he was the only man I had ever slept with, and I started sucking him again. This time it came up a little more, and again I crawled on top, but as I inserted his cock, he began to talk again. I put my hand over his mouth and said, "Now, shut up!" And guess what? He came within three strokes. I certainly didn't get any physical satisfaction out of it, but it was a real "moral" triumph—what a premature-postmature ejaculator!

In spite of the semihappy ending, this was a typical example of a common cause of impotence, and it has nothing to do with age. It's the anticipation of failure through fear of inadequate performance. Sex therapists call it performance anxiety, and in the absence of extensive treatment, they have a simple piece of advice: be a coward. They advise that a man not go to bed with a girl unless he really feels up to it and wants to. Don't go to bed with her if you're intimidated by her superior sexual status, or because you think it's expected of you, or because you want to be able to tell your buddies that you scored. Doctors believe that if men have sex only when they are really moved to, a great deal of impotence would disappear.

Impotence is described by therapists as a disruption of sexual function in the male that prevents satisfactory intercourse, and they believe that probably no other medical condition is as potentially frustrating, humiliating, or devastating to a man. Impotence can be an inability to get it up or to keep it up. Masters and Johnson describe two kinds of impotence: primary and secondary.

The man with primary impotence has had a problem getting a firm erection right from the beginning of his sex life, although he still may succeed at times or with certain special forms of stimulation. As an example of the first type, there was a very talented musician I knew who married a beautiful young woman performer. She soon discovered that her husband was a closet queen and, as it turned out, a "water-closet" queen, at that. Before he could get it up for her he had to disappear into the bathroom with a naked-muscleman-stud magazine to get aroused. Then, as soon as he got it nice and stiff, he would dash into the bedroom and fuck her before he had a chance to lose it again. The man with secondary impotence develops his erectile difficulty later in life, following a history of effective sexual functioning.

One cause of impotence that I've heard about from several wives is just plain lousy technique. A man should check out his style of lovemaking before deciding that he is impotent. The man who always makes love in the same position has an underlying emotional problem, because the normal psychosexuality of the male involves a lot of fantasy that this man must be suppressing.

Another frequent cause of impotence is sexual guilt. This can be based on associating sexual stimulation with a negative childhood experience, or it could be caused by parental mishandling of the child's sex development. Religion can be another cause; in other words, sex equals sin equals guilt.

A basically bad relationship or incompatibility between a couple, where the husband and wife have an underlying hostility to each other, whether they realize it or not, is very likely to give him soft-on problems. Frequently a woman is a bit of a prude and doesn't know, or want to know, how to respond to her lover's needs. Or perhaps he doesn't know how to ask, and this too can lead to eventual impotence. If a man requires oral sex to get it up, why make him go to a hooker to get laid? I'd go even further. If the man wants to get spanked, his wife should do it if that's what it takes to turn him on. The same thing goes for bondage.

I grant that a lot of men's sexual fantasies are based on having a submissive, innocent little girl at their sexual beck and call, but this is fantasy only. In reality, I believe the worst thing a woman can do in bed is play the virgin or the prude. A man wants a responsive, innovative woman who knows how to handle him and can do it without being overly aggressive, especially if he has problems. It's difficult to teach people this message, because it depends on intuition.

The only thing worse than mishandling a man in bed is not handling him at all. When I was working as a prostitute I talked to many men who came to me complaining that they were virtually chased out of their homes because the wives were having a kaffee klatch or a meeting of the PTA or had become involved in careers and couldn't cope with marriage as well. What happens is that, without becoming a widower, the husband suffers from the "widower's syndrome," when through the loss of his partner he stops fucking for a long period of time. If he waits too long, he may discover he has an energy crisis in his penis—that he can't easily start up again. There's a widely believed myth among some men that too much action uses up all his "come," as I mentioned before, or maybe wears out his penis, but the exact opposite is the truth. Practice makes perfect, and the man who fucks all his life will continue to fuck all his life!

Another thing that worries men about the power of their penis is the so-called male menopause, a time of life when they decide age is catching up and their sex life is getting ahead of them. The fact is that, around the late forties or early fifties, there may be a gradual decline in the male-hormone level, but it's not critical, and a man can still fuck and make babies as long as he can insert his penis into a vagina and come. Doctors say that although a man may lose a little of his sexual energy during this period, male menopause is mostly in his mind. So it's wrong to think that when you hit fifty you've had it, since it all depends on the individual. Just stay in shape, play a lot of tennis or participate in some other exercise, do a lot of yoga if you like, and stay in condition physically and sexually.

It's amazing how some men can turn impotent for a certain period of their lives, say during their sixties and seventies, and actually lose all interest in sex and maybe turn senile, and then, all of a sudden, their sex urge is aroused again, like a second adolescence. One often hears of cases of an old man chasing the nurse or grabbing the maid's tits. Maybe they realize it's now or never. It is said that certain drugs, like L-Dopa, for Parkinson's disease, have an ingredient that stimulates the sex drive; when it was first introduced a few years ago, doctors were puzzled to see all of the old buggers jump out of their wheelchairs and try to lay the nurses.

I noticed, when I had the brothel, that a lot of businessmen started to get old before their time sexually, sometimes when they hit forty, especially if they were the kind of men who did nothing but sit behind desks all day. I had a boyfriend when I was eighteen; he was twenty-eight, and he was great in bed, though a bit careless, and I actually got pregnant by him. When I saw him ten years later, at thirty-eight, he was a lousy lover. He had let himself go, he was overweight and flabby, and he just went through the motions. This proved to me that chronological age and sexual age are two different things. It wasn't the ten years that made the difference. It was mental and physical self-neglect.

To prove the point, I've had two septuagenarian lovers who have been as virile as any twenty-five-year-old stud. One of them is a famous show-business personality, a comedian who is always on the late talk shows. He's in his late seventies but still dates girls twenty to thirty-five. He even patronizes hookers frequently, always treating them like ladies. With me, it was a real affair. He's very romantic, a true gentleman of the old European style; he would kiss my hand, open doors, and was always courtly and attentive. He would tell me, "I'll take you away. Where do you want to go? Don't worry about a thing—I'll arrange for your visa papers." He was full of well-meant promises, and he had all the right connections. He had only one fault. He kept asking me, "Do you love me? Would you marry me?" I don't mind if a man says, "I love you." That's fine. But if I don't love the man, it's kind of hard for me to say, "Yes, I love you." But this man was so old and so gallant that I didn't want to hurt his feelings, so that part got to be a bit of a trial.

Anyway, after we had dated four or five times, the evening came when it seemed obvious we would be going to bed together. He was in New York from California and was staying in a big suite at a beautiful hotel. To tell you the truth, though, I wasn't looking forward to it too much. He was alert and well preserved, but he couldn't disguise the fact that he had a very old face. I expected some shriveled-up little penis that would require all kinds of acrobatics on my part to get it up. Some older men can get a semihard-on and are capable of coming, but they can't really insert it unless you're lubricated and you sit right on top of it. However, I had already noticed that this man had nice firm hands and a good strong handshake. His walk was very decisive, rather stiff, but not a feeble shuffle by any means. We got into bed and I started sucking his cock. I can tell you, it was plenty stiff; in fact, he had one of the nicest, firmest, biggest, cleanest cocks I have ever sucked. We had a very pleasant time in bed, and it even called for several encores later. He'll probably continue having a delightful and vigorous sex life for many years to come and may even die in the saddle. My guess is that that's the only way he'd want to go.

Another man who was in fantastic shape for his age was a person they call the Prince of Acapulco. He's in his early seventies. He's very athletic, playing tennis every day. At first I wasn't physically turned on by him, because he seemed quite a bit too old for me. But he persuaded me to come up to his beautiful home south of the border. I was barely settled in my room when he started drawing me a Japanese bath. He didn't join me in the sunken square-shaped bath, but he started rubbing my back with a soft soapy sponge, and he did it just beautifully. Then he wrapped me in an oversized towel and took me to his fantastic canopied bed. There was an exquisite Chopin nocturne playing, to put me in the right mood, and he started giving me a good, sensuous, deep massage.

Meanwhile, I had not yet seen his cock, and I didn't know if it was pink, green, or pinstriped, big or small. He was sitting on my buttocks, when I felt his towel drop away, and there was this tremendously big cock rubbing between my buttocks. With all that body lotion he was using, it was very smooth, and before I knew what was happening, he inserted his penis in my vagina and took me from the back. It felt like a strong young man making love to me, and it was beautiful. He was gentle and tender and virile, and one of the best lovers I've had in a long time.

Strangely enough, there are some men who have an energy crisis of another kind—the ones who have trouble getting it down. I'm not talking about the priapism problem but about perfectly normal men who take an unusually long time to detumesce, that is, for the blood to disengorge the penis after sex and allow it to drop back. Some men detumesce almost immediately after screwing, and some penises are still standing up, and practically lighting up, like a lamppost half an hour later.

This isn't too serious, of course. It's the Reluctant Penis we're concerned with. Therapists treating problems of the penis advise all males troubled with impotence to undergo a complete neurological and physical examination. Usually it's one of the more common psychological problems, but sometimes it's a physical one.

There are several medical conditions that can cause impotence. One is diabetes, and some men walk around with this illness undiagnosed, wondering why they can't get it up as easily as they once did. Other physical causes are: obesity, syphilis, certain kinds of prostatic surgical procedures, and injury to the spinal nerve that carries the message from the brain to the penis and tells it to stand up and get ready for action. Still other physical causes—and yet, numerous as they are, it is the psychological problems that are responsible for by far the greatest number of cases of impotence—are a certain form of epilepsy that affects the temporal lobe of the brain, multiple sclerosis, liver functioning problems, the use and abuse of various drugs, and the excessive use of alcohol.

Masters and Johnson, the world's foremost pioneers in the successful treatment of sex dysfunction, say secondary impotence is a reversible problem for all men, regardless of age. They have a cure rate of over ninety percent, based on the use of the famous "sensate focus" and the "squeeze technique."

Sensate focus is more or less teaching a couple to know each other's bodies, their erogenous zones, and what approach pleases the partner most. They are instructed over a period of several days to stroke each other only, all over their naked bodies, but not to have intercourse. This reduces any feeling of urgency or anxiety on the part of the man.

The squeeze technique is used to help eradicate the patient's fear of failure—that is, that if he loses his erection before or during intercourse he'll never be able to get it back, that the hard-on he has at the moment may be his last. The couple are told that when the man is as stiff as he usually gets, the woman is to squeeze the base quite firmly until the erection disappears. Then she stimulates his penis again, and he starts becoming a little more confident that what goes down can again come up.

Getting back to Amateur Night: there are quite a few things a woman does, consciously or unconsciously, that make her lover incapable of getting it up or cause him to lose it during lovemaking. From the thousands of men I have known and spoken to about what turns them off, I've compiled "Xaviera's Dirty Dozen Passion Killers" list. Most of these "don'ts" are not key contributors to serious cases of impotence, but they certainly don't help.

1. The woman who chain-smokes is definitely a sexual turn-off. She has to have the last puff before making love, and immediately afterward fumbles around on the night table to find her cigarettes and light up again.

2. The chatterbox is another accessory to a soft-on. She talks all the time—yak, yak, yak, yak—even in bed, to the point of continuing even when the man is performing oral sex on her. Variations of this are the woman with a grating, loud, or nasal voice—and the giggle freak.

3. Other sounds men find jarring and distracting are: excessively loud music played either on the radio or the stereo, the television news turned up loud in the background, and noisy beds. Unless a man gets a bang out of banging the bejesus out of a squeaky bed, you're better off moving to the sofa or to the floor.

4. Messy underwear, especially if it's worn out or pinned together, bra straps peeking out of one's sleeves, stockings with holes, greasy ungroomed hair, and personal items strewn around, such as hair curlers or soiled Kleenex, are turn-offs.

5. Excess hair is one of the worst turn-offs of all. When I was eighteen I had four or five hairs sprouting from my breasts, and I was so embarrassed that I just preferred to fuck without taking my bra off; finally I got wise and had the hair removed by electrolysis. A New York electrologist once told me she is constantly amazed when a woman confides to her, "My husband asked me to have it removed." The question is, why on earth did she wait that long?

6. The clock-watcher is more of a pain-in-the-ass than a sensation in the penis. General lack of concentration is boring enough, but when she says, "I wonder what time the next train back to town leaves?" or "Are you sure I can get a taxi out of here?"—just as they're about to get down to brass tacks—it makes him wonder why he asked her in the first place.

7. The compliment-seeker drives men mad—and not with desire, either. She constantly wants reassurance: "Am I as good as your other girlfriends?" "Am I as good as your wife?"

8. The comparison shopper is another unfailing passion killer. She talks all the time about previous lovers, and then indirectly lets slip the notion that the incumbent is very nice but not quite as big or as versatile.

9. The stage manager is a drag. She changes position constantly, on the mistaken assumption that she is pleasing him. Meanwhile, the energy he needs for screwing her is being used up trying to keep up with each new twist and turn.

10. The overreactor should probably take a tranquilizer. She goes off noisily on her own excited trip, gasping and screaming all over the place. Men would prefer it if she had a little more emotional control.

11. The underreactor should, on the other hand, swallow a bag of Mexican jumping beans. She's the woman who just lies there like a beached whale while he does all the work.

12. The "emcee" could use a course in q.t. She says, "Quick, honey, I'm coming, I'm coming, please come with me!" It's exciting at the beginning, but if the poor bugger just can't come that quickly, he'll lose

confidence in himself and might also lose something else, such as his erection.

Those are the "don'ts." How about the "dos"? If the man has an occasional attack of the soft-ons, there are various things a woman can try that may get it up in style. You might call this an "If All Else Fails" list.

1. Hop in a bath together beforehand; it's an emotional as well as a physical relaxer.

2. Have one or two—but no more—drinks, preferably wine or champagne.

3. Caress him a lot with his clothes on before getting stripped and getting down to it.

4. Leave on an item or two of clothing or jewelry while making love.

5. Good, warm mouth work has been known to perform wonders.

6. Develop an instinct for pacing, trying to reach the same points of stimulation or arousal together. Know each other's rhythm.

7. If the penis is being stubborn in bed, say, "Okay, I'll play with myself, and you play with yourself." After five or ten minutes of this no-pressure activity, you might very well spot a full erection out of the corner of your eye.

8. Someone recently told me that if it really won't budge, a woman should slap her lover's soft penis very hard, and the shock will make it rise to the occasion. I would consider this an extreme measure indeed, and for all my boldness, I've never tried it. Somehow I have the feeling that I just might knock it down forever. But if someone has enough nerve to try it, I'd like to know how it works. I'm still learning.

CHAPTER SIXTEEN

Sex Appeal Seventies Style, OR, My Most Penetrating Performers

Sex appeal, in a way, is like money—you've either got it or you haven't. You can't legitimately steal or copy it, and it is subject to wildly inflated values. It's the stuff legends—and too many myths—are made of, underestimated by some, overestimated by others, and misunderstood by many. Sex appeal is *not* just another pretty face, a bedroom technique, a big penis, or any other tangible asset. It is a combination of any of those things plus personal style. Yet, what too many men do not realize is that most of them have the potential to increase their share—with interest!

One of the biggest myths concerning sex appeal is the cliché of the Latin lover. So many men, nervous with eleventh-hour jitters, have said to me, "I bet you prefer the Latin-lover type." Nothing could be further from reality. The truth of the matter is, of all the categories of male sex appeal, dear old Don Juan is the dullest. This man, with his smoldering looks, lyricism about the stars and the moon, irrational jealousies, dedication to the double standard, and obsession with marrying a virgin, is to love what the Studebaker is to the automobile industry—obsolete. He is "tyrannasaurus sex"!

In these liberated times, possessiveness is ridiculous, *machismo* a bore—nobody needs an egomaniac—and *crime passionnel* is a pain, in more ways than one. The Latin lover may be great sexually, which is good news for women who just want or need an adventure for kicks. The American schoolteacher who goes to Spain or south of the border for a vacation will find him a great tourist attraction. She is flattered by the pinch, the whistle, or the compliment, the way he helps her into her coat or holds a door open. But what she does not realize is that she is being used as a doormat. These men don't really care what makes her tick as a woman; they whistle at anything that walks, as long as she's a woman, preferably blond and perhaps with a nice suntan. Even my own dear mother, who recently came back from a vacation in Marbella, told me she was approached by several Spanish would-be lovers. I'm not saying she's not attractive, and a superb person, but she definitely is the sweet motherly type.

The Latin lover has a long way to go as far as his behavior toward women and his attitude toward modern sexuality is concerned. He demands that a woman stay home and be faithful, yet he continually is inventing excuses to go out with the boys, or out on the town. In his book *The Original Sin*, that lovable Mr. Machismo of the screen, Anthony Quinn, talks about the night he married a woman several years his senior, after having lived with another older woman for some years. He found out, on his wedding night, he says, that his wife was not a virgin, so he slapped her face and left her. To me this shows there is something deeply wrong with this man's attitude toward women and sexuality. And he is only *half* Mexican!

If all this sounds somewhat uncharitable, as though I am rejecting an entire category of male out of hand, I can say that one of the most fantastic lovers I ever had was a Mexican. This man was young, handsome, rich, gentlemanly, tender, and very deep. He was a racing-car driver who gave all his winnings to the poor, and there was a vein of generosity throughout his entire character. However, he felt very awkward about being in the house of prostitution I was running at the time, and insisted on privacy. In other words, he waited until everybody had gone and I switched off the phones. Then he would make love to me all over the room, on the bed, the carpet, against the vanity table, and in the bathroom. He was very experienced for a man who had told me, and I believed him, that he had cheated on his wife only twice in six years of marriage. On the other hand, he told me if he ever caught her cheating he would kill her!

If the Latins are no longer *numero uno* as lovers, what nationality replaced them? Amazingly, it's a group of men which as recently as five or six years ago I would never have regarded as candidates for any prize in sex appeal. This group consists of Germans, Austrians, and middle Europeans—Czechs, Yugoslavs, and Hungarians. (The Swiss, unfortunately for them, are excluded from this group.) Swiss men are known to be stingy, stubborn, and humorless, and are unable to conduct a lighthearted or frivolous conversation.

This new group of international lovers, especially the younger Germans and Austrians who immigrate to the United States and Canada, have a certain touch of class. They have retained old-fashioned charm, and I don't mean something as superficial as standing up when a lady has to leave the table or opening the car door for her. It's the paying of the sincere compliment, the consideration of bringing her flowers or a box of chocolates, or just making her feel very right about herself that counts. There's something romantic and sensitive about these gestures, because they express thoughtfulness. Even if some of these men are not really very attractive physically, their courteous behavior makes them Adonises in a woman's eyes. This kind of man knows that genuine consideration will get him much farther with a woman—whether for a one-night encounter or something more lasting—than a demanding or neglectful attitude.

One of the best lovers I have had in my entire life was a man in this category, a Hungarian. This man, by the way, was monumental proof that the young stud is not necessarily the answer to every maiden's dreams. Alexander was, from a technical point of view, the best lover I have ever had, and he taught me more about sex in one night than any other I had ever known. I should explain that, in this situation, the attraction was purely sexual; but even though we had no intention of falling in love with each other, it certainly was not one of those slam-bam-thank-you-ma'am deals. Alexander was a very charming man of the European school who knew how to warm up my sexual appetite during the evening as we wined and dined. His conversation touched on group sex, bisexuality, and sexual activities with other women. But this conversation lasted only until we arrived at his house; once we were in his bedroom, he made me feel as if I were the Queen of the Night and that I was the only one who counted. In other words, "Alexander the Great" got into my head before I got into his bed.

The outstanding thing about him was that although he was quite a big man, he was as agile as Nureyev and could assume many positions. It was not only the thirteen or so exciting new positions he showed me, but the way in which he moved his body as he changed into them. He was not, however, one of those acrobatic types who try to impress you with impossible physical performances. Technically speaking, I would have to rate this man as the best lover I have *ever* had, and I would like to find another one like him, because try as I did to duplicate Alexander's techniques with other lovers, he had taken his erotic secrets with him.

Another category of male that tremendously appeals to me is what I call the "earthy" type. You cannot easily define this man in physical terms, because many, many men have some of the earthy qualities and yet have nothing in common with each other. The earthy man, first of all, is not necessarily handsome. In fact, he is more likely to be homely, or even actually ugly, than he is to be a screen idol like Robert Redford. But there is a ruggedness about him, and he doesn't care too much about outward appearances. He's certainly no slob, but he is also no tailor's dummy who spends hours over which multicolored shirt, suede pants, or fancy cologne to wear. As far as his car goes, he is more likely to tool around in a beat-up Volkswagen than a flashy sports car, because he's very secure as a man.

The earthy type of man I've met is usually outgoing, spontaneous, and charming, but not in a superficial way. In other words, he does not come on with the same old idle party chatter, but usually has something more original and more genuine to say. Hopefully, he has a sense of humor, and he has one other thing that a lot of men definitely lack: a certain animal quality. A person can develop charm and a certain amount of sex appeal, but not the basic sexual instinct. I believe this is something you are born with, and in my case, I knew what sexuality was all about as far back as I can remember. The earthy man knows intuitively about sex, but generally doesn't talk about it. Merely by his general conduct one can assume he is a good bed partner.

Quite often, maturity deepens this earthy quality. Suffering and life experience also add to it and make a person more compassionate, less nervous, and more sure of himself. After all, a face, and particularly that of a man, only becomes interesting when you can read it like a road map.

If this kind of man has a weakness at all, it does not show—but it comes through as a sort of softness about his character. In public, this man may not even show his affection, and at a party he may choose to be completely independent, saying, "You go your way—I'll go my way." But yet, you know, through one touch when he walks by, or the meeting of eyes across a room, that this is your man—if you're lucky. Even the squarest woman will fall for the earthy type of man, and he is a great second lover to have around if a woman has a man at home who doesn't quite satisfy her needs as far as the animalistic urge goes. She can even use him as a fantasy that need never be fulfilled, but just employed to charge up her batteries (the so-called "zipless fuck"). Paradoxically, this type, who for my taste oozes sex appeal, can sometimes be a zilch as a lover. Strangely enough, this does not really discourage you from enjoying him.

One of the greatest sexual episodes I had recently was with an earthy type of man, and it was really a "nonfuck." It happened with a man who was rather a special close friend. He had become annoyed at something I did, and justifiably so. To punish me, he decided to go on strike and withhold sex from me until the end of the month, which was a very long two weeks away. For the first five days we were together, he kissed me, kissed my breasts, turned me on tremendously, and got huge hard-ons himself. But he refused to take off his pants, or to eat me, or give me any satisfaction.

By the sixth day we were driving each other crazy, because neither had masturbated to relieve the sexual tension, so we climbed into bed during the afternoon, and pretty soon our underwear disappeared and we started teasing each other almost to death. My "striking" lover refused to eat me, but he slipped his big, hard penis between the outer lips of my vagina, which were full and swollen with excitement. My clitoris was throbbing and standing up. I sucked him for a while, almost to the point of no return; then I stopped and rubbed him against my breasts before sucking him again. His hands caressed my body and vagina, but he still refused to go any further. Eventually we became so excited that we almost pulled the trigger on the spot, so we decided to stop then and there. That night, under a shower to cool our passion, we soaped each other all over, with me rubbing his penis against my clitoris, and he, at the same time, putting one finger up my anus and another up my vagina. And that way we both had a nonfuck orgasm. He continued withholding sex from me for yet another week to make his point and teach me a lesson, and I must say that nonfuck was one of the most exciting, if frustrating, experiences I had had in a long time.

Yet another category of man is the one I would describe as the truly square, straight male. In sexual terms, this means he doesn't really care for oral, anal, or group sex. He thinks bisexuality is having sex every two years, and around the world is what you win on *The Dating Game*. In general appearance and style he either belongs to the Brooks Brothers button-down-shirt set, and wears a three-piece pinstripe suit. This man is the button-down lover—you have to literally peel him out of his shell, as well as his clothes. When I ran my house of prostitution in New York I met many of these men as customers. Professionally, he is probably an investment banker, stockbroker, or business executive. Socially, he can talk at length on how to invest your money; but in a lighthearted conversation or a discussion about the arts, he usually strikes out. The possible exception to this category type-casting is the top-echelon Harvard- or Yale-educated business executive who comes from a well-established, well-connected WASP family. A man like this was probably married young to a woman with the same financial and social background; she may be quite frigid and probably lives up in Connecticut. With this man there is often something potentially earthy, as I found in one memorable affair I had back in those days. This man, a bank president, was what you might call a weekend husband. That means Saturdays and Sundays with the wife and kids, and the weekdays in his pad downtown. I fell madly in love with him—

his name was Dermot—and he treated me, even though I was a madam, with a great deal of love and respect. He would take me shopping, buy me clothes, and take me to the theater if I could find the time to go. He was tolerant as far as my business was concerned, although I know he didn't like the fact that I had other men while he was there. He sort of looked the other way and entertained the girls, not with his body but with his mind and his intelligent conversation. And he had something that was rather exceptional for the button-down boys, a sense of humor. My banker's sexual specialty was the so-called tree position, where I would stand on the bed while he would stand beside it with his erect penis at a ninety-degree angle so that I could slowly slide on top of it and wrap my legs around the waist of his well-proportioned body. He enjoyed walking around the bed with me that way, stopping now and then to lay me on my back and penetrate me deeper. Then he would ask me to sit on top of him, sometimes assisted by another girl, and gyrate around his penis, somewhat like they do in the Japanese basket fuck. (This is an Oriental whorehouse specialty in which a naked girl sits in a special rattan chair suspended by ropes from the ceiling while the client lies below on his back on a pillow, with his erect penis in the air; another two girls then lower her dangling cunt over his penis and gyrate the chair, giving the man what must be an exquisite sensation.) However, with my not-so-button-down lover, I was quite happy with only the assistance of one or two of my girls who helped me enjoy him that way.

A category of males capable of mental as well as physical stimulation are those involved in the entertainment business. These men are in constant contact with interesting people and events and are, by definition, real performers. The ones I like usually dress conservatively, but with flair, and are, as dates, unpredictable enough not to be boring. One such man was a well-known television personality in New York who was a light-skinned Negro from Martinique. I developed a sort of Electra complex toward him, because in many ways he reminded me of my father. Not that my father was black, but they had similar features, and Charles had the same brand of wit and intelligence. As a lover, his performance was Academy Award caliber. He was well equipped and he had marvelous agility. This man could move his pelvic area, from his waist to his groin, completely independently of the rest of his body, in such a way that his weight never touched me. Actually, as far as technique went, he was rather conventional, but the few positions he did know sure made up for it. My favorite position was to lie on my back with a pillow underneath me while he was on his knees teasing my vagina with his penis, flicking it back and forth until I begged him to put it inside me. I would have my legs circled around his waist so I could more easily push him in and out of me. When a woman has her legs around her lover's shoulders, it makes her a little bit helpless as far as movement goes; while his penis penetrates deeper, it's not really as sensual. Another thing about Charles, the performer, was the way his penis was constantly oozing, so that it was always nicely lubricated. And the way he could make love to me with his tender, velvety eyes at the same time he was fucking me was one more thing that made him memorable as a lover.

Another category of men is the so-called hairy-chested truck driver or construction worker. Men in this category usually underestimate themselves in terms of sex appeal. This group often feels they cannot compete with others because of a certain lack of refinement. This is not true in view of what they have going for them, provided they have the sort of pride in their appearance that the ones I have known possessed. They have a natural animal quality that, if they could package it, would make a fortune. Some of the world's most sexually knowledgeable women have preferred the truck-driver type as lovers; feminist-fatale Germaine Greer, for example, married a construction worker. From my experience, I have enjoyed the spontaneity and energy of the blue-collar set, and one of my most exciting recent lovers was a construction-worker apprentice—with a great future. His name was Terry and he was the eighteen-year-old son of a famous artist in Toronto, about whom I had been fantasizing for a couple of years but who, because he was true to his wife, remained an impossible dream. However, one day the father called me up to say his son, Terry, who lived in a whistlestop town in New Jersey, was coming to visit and needed to be inaugurated. Since I couldn't make the grade with the father, I decided to penetrate this attractive family via the son.

One afternoon I went over to their house, which was a spacious and opulently decorated waterfront apartment, where Terry was waiting with a young friend of his. They were obviously both virgins and terribly shy, so I made the first move by suggesting we all get stoned on grass cigarettes smeared with hash oil. That made us fly so high that I had to remind myself that I had been asked to take care of the son. Not knowing whether this young boy was circumcised or not, but not wanting to ruin the atmosphere of the occasion by asking, I ran a full, foamy bath, and we both climbed into it and sat looking at each other and stroked each other's bodies. I did everything I could conceivably do in the tub—soaping him, stroking him, entering him with my finger—and he exploded within a couple of minutes. Aware that he was very young, I knew there was more to come. And as much as his father was a true intellectual, this kid was a rugged individual who would one day be a real sexual animal if he allowed his instincts to develop naturally. In a little while we dried ourselves and got into bed. I was really amazed at how beautiful his body was; it was muscular but not too sinewy, and he had a natural grace of movement. I taught him first to do sixty-nine; he started to kiss the wrong spots, putting his tongue all the way into my vagina. I gently directed his head to my clitoris, and once he found it, he sucked it as well as the most experienced of my lovers. He took it in his lips like a little penis and made me come almost instantly. Then, when we actually got down to fucking, which only went as far as the missionary style, he performed like a thoroughbred stallion. I felt sorry for his friend, who had to sit around and watch—getting figuratively deflowered—but I can say that taking care of my friend's construction-worker son was definitely a labor of love.

Another category of men—full of surprises—is that of the artist and writer. These men, who often appear remote and aloof, are often sizzling sexualists when behind closed doors. Naturally, being creative people, they are usually very sensual and certainly never lacking in imagination.

One man I knew, a well-known novelist and a sometime client of mine in New York, used to like having call girls drop by the luxurious apartment he shared with his mistress on Central Park South. It had a big round bed, with a ceiling mirror above it. His mistress, however, was frequently away overseas, and his big kick was to make a transatlantic call to her while he was making it with one of us. This man was one of the best fucks I've ever had, not so much in terms of technique as because of the fantasy atmosphere he created. He had one of those amplification telephones in his bedroom, the kind that need not be hand-held, and he would turn this on when the girl arrived. He'd call up his mistress and start telling her, in very erotic detail, what he would love to be doing to her at the time, while all the while he was doing it to me. She would reply in the same way, and I would not be surprised if she were making it with a guy at the other end. For creative lovemaking, this artist was hard to beat.

A category of male who can usually handle himself well in social as well as sexual situations is the professional—the lawyer, doctor, or dentist, who deals with people's problems and who therefore understands them reasonably well. Because of his profession, this man is in the habit of dressing fairly conservatively but nicely. With few exceptions, professional men are quite predictable and rarely let a woman down. One such man I knew was a twenty-six-year-old dentist of Turkish extraction; he was fantastic with oral work and a real specialist at filling cavities. His name was

Salah, and because he had a steady girlfriend when we first met, he walked around with me with a hard-on for a year until the opportunity to make love came around.

It happened, finally, in circumstances that were far from ideal, and certainly not romantic. It was at an orgy where there was too much bright light and too many other people. However, when Salah, who had a long, silky-smooth tongue, started making love to me, we forgot everybody else and gave such a star performance that at the end we received a round of applause from our audience. Salah's great skill was in oral work. He kissed me sensually all over my body, my toes, my calves, the backs of my knees, thighs, around the world, eventually penetrating my vagina with his tongue, which performed like a small, skillful penis, and was a true Turkish delight!

Another category, that of the athlete or jock, is envied by many men. They see athletes as magnificent physical specimens who have no trouble attracting women and winning them as sexual fans. However, this is not necessarily the case. It's true that they look good, have a glamorous profession, and are surrounded by camp followers, or "groupies," who are willing to share their beds with no guarantee that the guy will even remember their name in the morning. However, their problem is living up to their own image, and this tends, in my experience, to intimidate many of them. Also, while they may look great physically, they too often fail sartorially.

When I had my whorehouse, I had lots of athletes, usually members of out-of-town teams, who felt entitled to treat themselves to a night of sex as a victory prize, especially since many of them were away from their wives and kids. They would arrive as a team, dressed in the worst-put-together outfits of wine-red double-knit checkered slacks, midnight-blue blazers, and yellow shirts. Some of them would wear those high heels, which look ridiculous on a man with a frame like a boxer; they look much better on slim-assed guys. But more important, when the evening got down to the naked truth, they weren't as well endowed as their reputations make them seem.

Certainly the jock didn't start the myth that he is hung like a stallion. Nevertheless, a myth is all it is. Then too, I've found that the jock's excellence in sport is on the playing field, not in the bedroom. This is partly because he would genuinely rather be home with his wife and kids than in some strange city and some strange whorehouse, but it's not considered team spirit to say so. In that frame of mind, they sometimes arrive for a wild night in a brothel, with an ego as fragile as a paper cup and a performance that's just as hollow.

My most memorable athletic experience was when the Israeli soccer team visited Johannesburg, long before I became a prostitute and we were all at a typically boring South African party. I have always liked Israelis, despite their arrogance, because they are strong, energetic, and swarthy. These guys were all raunchy-looking and all just as bored with the evening as I was. So I suggested that we pile into a couple of cars and drive into town to buy some fried chicken. Needless to say, we stopped off in a park by the road, and one by one I fucked and sucked the seven who came on the expedition. This made me very much hornier than I was when we set out. When we returned to the party, the word went around, quietly but very quickly, among the other four. So I had them, one by one, in the host's bathroom.

A category of men, familiar to all, and underestimated by many, is the tweed-and-corduroy, pipe-smoking intellectual. This man, who is often dismissed as being more interested in science than sex, is in fact a whole encyclopedia of exciting formulas. The quiet, bookish academic is often the personification of the saying "still waters run deep."

Recently, in Toronto, I had a memorable experience with a professor of English at Toronto University, named Crispin, who was married to another professor. Once or twice I had invited the couple to parties at my apartment, but Crispin would turn up alone. He looked sort of incongruous in a room full of swingers, but this would not stop him from sitting back, smoking his pipe, which had a lovely toffee smell—sometimes pipe tobacco can be repulsive, but his was attractive—and joining in whatever conversation was going on, no matter what the subject. Throughout the night I would see him watching me in a warm, admiring way. At the end of the evening I would take him down in the elevator and kiss him innocently on the cheek. However, during this recent occasion, I was flattered by the way he was watching me all night, so I became a little flirtatious. Then, when he announced he had to leave early, I took him down in the elevator and decided, in a spirit of mischief, to tongue-kiss him. I was wearing a wraparound dress at the time, with nothing on underneath, and just to shock him, I let it fall open and pressed against his body. With the reaction of a jailer, he reached over my shoulder and pressed the stop button of the elevator, opened the door, and pulled me through the door that led onto the stairwell. Without bothering to say anything, he turned me to face the banister, lifted my dress from behind, and penetrated me, rather roughly, as he repeated an exciting litany of just what had been going through his mind as he smilingly watched me playing hostess at my parties.

Probably the most envied category of lovers is the man who makes a sport out of it—the playboy. This guy has style, experience, access to beautiful women, and enough money and time to take advantage of it. However, successful and enviable as he might be from a man's point of view, as far as a woman is concerned he is so preoccupied with the pursuit that he wouldn't recognize the perfect woman for him even if he found her. There was one famous case of the Brazilian playboy who married a beautiful young heiress who had been sought by half of the eligible bachelors in Europe. However, he was too much a prisoner of his own desires to settle down and enjoy his lot, so much so that one night he told her he was going out for some cigarettes. To this day, he has never bothered to return home.

I had a scene in Europe with an international playboy named Paul, who was typical of this type. He was a manufacturer of high-fashion clothing and had a factory in Paris and exclusive boutiques in the watering spots of Europe, including St. Tropez, which was where I met him. Paul was certainly elegant and attractive, drove a powerful sports car, and dated the most beautiful women around. All this man had to do was snap his fingers and the women would fly to his bed like homing pigeons.

From the women who had a crush on him, I found out he never slept with the same one twice, so I conditioned myself not to fall in love but to see him as a good fuck for the evening, the way many men see women. When my turn came around to be invited to his bed, I learned that the playboy knew his craft well, because, as aloof and indifferent as he seemed on the outside, he was a warm, passionate, and very inventive lover in bed. He had tremendous endurance, could come three or four times during the evening, and was an expert at knowing exactly what to say and how to make it sound genuine. In other words, he could make every woman believe, even though in her heart of hearts she knew better, that she was the only one for him. Because of his bedtime experience, Paul had gone far beyond basic in-and-out lovemaking. We did some of that, and it was not so much the size of his penis, which was rather slim and long, making it all the better for anal penetration, but the way he used it. He knew how to compensate in technique and make it tantalize the clitoris by hitting the right angle. Paul's great skill was the staging of the performance, and he took me on some kinky side trips. Once he gently gagged me, tied me over a few pillows, and penetrated me from the back. Later he put a leash around my neck and led me around the bed and fucked me that way. Then I reversed our roles and tied him into submission, making him beg like a puppy for more of my favors as I fastened his feet and arms behind his back and dripped hot wax on his balls. As I expected, we made no plans to meet again after that night, but when I did run into him at a big orgy, I was flattered that he selected me, along with another girl, as his partner for the marathon event.

From the long list of categories of men, you can see that one is not necessarily better than the other, just different, and that all have merit. That's why it's a mistake for, say, the construction worker to tell himself, "If I go out and buy leather pants, gold chains, get my hair cut in a different way, I'll be an instant swinger." That will only look ridiculous and convince no one. The advice I would give to a man who recognizes himself in one of these categories is: be yourself, don't try to imitate anyone else. Just try to develop your own style, personality, and approach to women. Bearing this in mind, the following is a *safe* and reliable list of Leg-Opener Dos and Don'ts for all men—from Xaviera with love.

1. Possibly the last man I would choose as my lover of the evening would be the first one who came over and struck up a shallow conversation. There's a "steamroller" in every crowd who comes on with all that irritating small talk: "What's your name, where are you working, do you live with your parents, can I call you sometime?" He sounds like he's checking out a piece of prime sirloin rather than an intelligent human being. He usually has a phony compliment about your appearance on the very night you know very well you look shitty. He then slips you his card and continues to monopolize your company, making it impossible for you to get to know the more worthwhile men in the room.

2. Reserved Ronald, on the other hand, can sometimes overdo the silent act. This, literally, is just

dumb. The most exciting man in any gathering keeps up a good conversation that is not shallow; he appears genuinely interested in you as a person, is entertaining but not a clown, and probably wants to get into your pants but is going to intrigue you by not showing his hand, or his penis, prematurely. I always believe that behind the conservative public display is a wealth of private passion.

3. Warm up your partner before you get home. A lot depends on how well you know her. Try running your hand through her hair at the cinema, or giving her a tender, spontaneous kiss on the neck or ear. Make sure it's sincere—you sincerely want to fuck her, don't you? At dinner, touch her leg under the table, or gently hold her hand. But don't be too persistent about it, don't overdo it, or maul or grope. And when you finally get her behind closed doors, don't pounce. Stay with the right set of signals.

4. Don't slobber, or be a slob. Don't drink too much, and if you smoke, slip away to brush your teeth or use a mouthwash before bedtime. Everyone knows by now that I prefer to talk my lover into a shower or bath, especially if we've been out all day or dancing all night.

5. Take the lead, even though it may be her house. If she has poured you the first drink, offer to pour her the next. Another thing I love is when a man offers to select the records at my house. Respect her privacy and don't drop in unannounced, unless you're one hundred percent sure she's alone and feeling presentable. Be discreet, don't demand to know everything she does, and don't suffocate the relationship. A man I know snuffed the life out of his marriage because he was so possessive that he forbade his new wife to see

any of her old friends. She was really in love with him but could not endure the restrictions he imposed on her individuality.

6. Often, when I'm at a book-signing party, a woman will come up with a pair of her husband's underpants for me to autograph. There are times when I fantasize erotically about the owner; however, this *never* happens in the case of those longish boxer shorts, especially the ones with hearts, flowers, or bumblebees printed all over them. Too-tiny bikinis can also look ridiculous, unless the man has an exceptionally good body. The sexiest underpants, in my opinion, are the modified abbreviated hipsters in solid colors or simple patterns.

7. The finger-fucker is one of the world's worst lovers. He is not so ignorant that he has not heard about foreplay, but his idea of a warmer-upper is to do a quick probe of her clitoris, then plunge his finger inside her vagina. Most women really hate having a finger suddenly thrust up their vagina or anus. Also, heavyhanded clitoral stimulation really hurts.

8. A lot of men are ignorant of the fact that proper clitoral stimulation is what really gets a woman off. It can be applied orally or digitally, if the man is gentle and knows what he is doing. There's a certain kind of man who thinks that if he puts his penis inside a woman's vagina, she will be satisfied. If she doesn't react, he automatically assumes she is frigid. However, I don't believe there is any woman who is really 100 percent frigid—it's usually the fault of a lousy lover and seldom that of physical disability. In some cases, frigidity is caused by strict upbringing and religious taboos. The selfish lover has probably never tried oral sex or gentle masturbation on his woman.

Neither does he know that, unless the penis rubs backward and forward in intercourse so that the clitoris is stimulated, the woman will probably not have an orgasm.

9. The Great Dictator is another pest. He lies back there like royalty and says, "Say, why don't you jerk me off?" Or, "Why don't you suck my cock ... or climb up and sit on my face?" My question to him is, why doesn't he go out and buy himself a plastic fuck doll that doesn't have desires of her own?

10. The pneumatic drill is, literally, a bore. He pumps away unimaginatively, with no variation whatsoever in speed or pressure. A change of pace that really excites me is for my lover to put it in for a while and then pull it out while I say, "No, stay inside me, don't leave me." Then he teases me for a few seconds before he puts it in again. The feather fucker, on the other hand, says, "Am I hurting you, am I too rough?" Meantime, he has about as much zest in his stroke as a mouse on a treadmill.

11. The wrestler and the acrobat both might be more at home in a gymnasium than in a bed. The wrestler suffocates you with a stranglehold that would leave Charles Bronson gasping for breath. The acrobat, on the other hand, wants twenty different positions, and always decides to change just when he has finally found the perfect one. To me, by the way, the most satisfying position for two people who are emotionally turned on to each other is the old-fashioned face-to-face. It is the most tender and most gratifying of all, particularly if the woman is on top and if the man's ego is not fragile. She can sit, squat, make a complete turn and face him with her bottom, stretch out her legs, or feed him her breasts.

12. The silent partner comes without letting anybody know. A man should at least make nice, loving sounds to let her share his orgasm. Then there's the hysteria freak, the one who roars the whole house down. It's nice to have an animal in bed sometimes, but it's better if he is house-trained and has some self-control. I once made love with a man who, when he came, laughed like a drunken hyena. This confused me, because I thought I had done something ridiculous until I realized this was just the normal expression of his passion.

13. In a long-lasting affair, be sensitive about the other person's needs. Don't reject her advances because "I'm watching television now, dear," and then tap her on the shoulder in the middle of the night when she's sound asleep. Never expect, never demand, and try to have your lovemaking times suit your mutual desires. And one last word—don't make a habit of rolling over and falling asleep immediately after sex. Women hate it—and will hate you for doing it. Do it once too often, and you'll wake up alone.

That really isn't the last word, of course. The last word on THE BEST PART OF A MAN and how it can be used for mutual satisfaction and pleasure will never be spoken. The penis is always up to something new and surprising, even for an old hand at the game. I for one look forward to new thrills ahead.

Author's Note

After quite some years of "penetrating" research, I believe that I deserve the title of expert "penologist," and that is why I decided to write this book on the penis, or the long and short of it.

Originally the title was meant to be "The Wonder Stick" or "Man's Best Friend," but since some readers might confuse "Man's Best Friend" with his dog, and bookstores might object to "The Wonder Stick," I came up with the title *The Best Part of a Man*. This title might have a slight female chauvinistic twist to it, but, then again, for ages man has considered woman as not much more than legs, bottoms, and boobs, so ... here we are: The best part of a man, or should I say, the most pleasurable part of a man, is in my opinion definitely his penis. Please forgive me, gentlemen, I realize there is much more to you guys than just that—like a mind, a brain, a soul. I hope we all have learned something from this book; if not ... keep an eye out for my next book, *Xaviera's Lessons in Love*. If you have any interesting stories to tell or suggestions about specific sexual escapades, please do not hesitate to write to Bernard Geis Associates, 128 East 56th Street, New York, New York 10022.